the
beach house cookbook

also by mary kay andrews

the
beach house cookbook

easy breezy recipes with a southern accent

mary kay andrews

ashley strickland freeman: food stylist and project editor
elizabeth demos: photo stylist and creative director
mary britton senseney: photographer

st. martin's press ❧ new york

THE BEACH HOUSE COOKBOOK. Copyright © 2017 by Whodunnit, Inc.
All rights reserved. Printed in the United States of America. For information, address
St. Martin's Press, 175 Fifth Avenue, New York, N.Y. 10010.

www.stmartins.com

Interior and endpapers designed by Kathryn Parise

Photographer: Mary Britton Senseney
Creative Director and Photo Stylist: Elizabeth Demos
Food Stylist, Recipe Tester, and Project Editor: Ashley Strickland Freeman

The Library of Congress Cataloging-in-Publication Data is available upon request.

ISBN 978-1-250-13044-0 (hardcover)
ISBN 978-1-250-13045-7 (e-book)

Our books may be purchased in bulk for promotional, educational, or business use. Please
contact your local bookseller or the Macmillan Corporate and Premium Sales Department at
1-800-221-7945, extension 5442, or by e-mail at MacmillanSpecialMarkets@macmillan.com.

First Edition: May 2017

10 9 8 7 6 5 4 3 2 1

Contents

Preface

The phrase "beach house" conjures up all kinds of magical images for me: morning walks along the shore, sun-splashed beach picnics, and outdoor showers followed by lazy late afternoons lolling in the shade, with yet one more foray back to the water late in the day. And then, for me the perfect beach house day is capped off with icy cocktails at sunset, followed by a dinner of fresh-caught seafood with sides of coleslaw and potato salad, thickly sliced tomatoes, and corn on the cob from the nearest farm stand, followed by a sinfully delicious dessert—lemon bars? Or maybe just a stroll down the block for ice cream or gelato from the neighborhood parlor. After dinner, my favorite activity is a spirited board game—Scrabble? Trivial Pursuit? Or my grandchildren's favorite, Yahtzee.

Growing up in St. Petersburg, Florida, as the second of five children, I lived a block away from Tampa Bay and thirty minutes away from the Gulf of Mexico beaches, but the idea of actually owning a beach house was considered "pie in the sky" for my hard-working parents.

However, for many years, we could, and did, rent a beach house for two glorious weeks every July. My family's preferred destination was a typical old-style Florida mom-and-pop tourist court called—and in retrospect, I love the irony—Ocee Villas, at Indian Rocks Beach on the Gulf of Mexico. Our "villa" was a one-story concrete-block affair of around 800 square feet, with two tiny bedrooms and a single bath. But it had air-conditioning, which our own home lacked, not to mention a pool; a recreation hall with a Ping-Pong table, juke box, and a vacuum cleaner motor–powered player piano; and best of all, a seemingly endless stretch of sugar-fine white beaches. Our rented beach cottage was probably only twenty-five miles from our house in "town," but to us, it was just as exotic a destination as the Italian Riviera.

My memory of the Ocee Villas is of sharing a rollaway bed or lumpy pullout sofa with my little sister, Patti, while Susie, the oldest in the family, got a bed of her own, and my younger brothers, Johnny and Timmy, were on twin beds in one bedroom, with my parents in the "master bedroom." Looking back now, I marvel that my mother— who did all the cooking in our family of seven—considered this a vacation. Especially since the kitchen at our "villa" consisted of a tiny apartment-size electric stove; a balky, undersize fridge; zero counter space; and an eccentric array of kitchenware. Still, Mom was always up for a challenge, and somehow she managed to feed us—and the hordes of assorted friends and relatives who dropped in at dinnertime—without turning a hair on her frosted, teased bouffant.

I'm sure we kids ate lots of baloney and peanut butter and jelly sandwiches—while Dad snacked on liverwurst and Ritz crackers, which he regarded as a vacation delicacy. I know we had a charcoal grill, and that we had hot dogs and hamburgers with mounds of sweet, vinegary coleslaw and creamy potato salad. And deviled eggs. Always deviled eggs. Dessert was probably a fresh peach cobbler Mom made from bruised fruit she culled at our neighborhood A&P and bought at a deep discount, or my father's favorite, banana pudding, or maybe a chocolate cake. The young'uns washed dinner down with cherry Kool-Aid, my mother sipped her beloved Nestea Instant Tea between chain-smoking Kools or Salems, and Dad had his Big Blue—Budweiser. We crowded around a Formica-topped table meant for a party of four, sunburnt, tired, chlorine-scented, and ravenous, and talked and teased and bickered until we fell into our beds, exhausted and already planning the next day's big adventure.

Today, the Ocee Villas are gone, long since replaced by high-rise hotels and condo towers. My parents and two of my siblings are also gone, and greatly mourned. Those simple, salt-scented beach house memories are ones I've sought to re-create ever since.

After I married my high school sweetheart, Tom, and we moved to Georgia and had two children of our own, we returned to those same Gulf beaches for many years, renting similar cottages.

Our beach house menus changed to suit our family. Because Tom is a gifted fisherman (I joke that he could catch a tarpon in a bathtub), our beach house meals usually included the day's catch: flounder, speckled trout, redfish, or—if he'd had a really good day—snook, which is a notoriously wily (and delicious) game fish.

When our children reached school age, we often spent their Easter break in the Florida Panhandle town of Grayton Beach. We'd descend en masse with several neighborhood families, renting huge homes that slept up to twenty people. Each family was assigned a night to prepare dinner for the crowd, with one night reserved for dinner out—usually at the Red Bar, a popular local hangout—and the last Saturday night was the assigned "clean out the fridge" night.

Ten years ago, after our children were grown and (mostly) gone, and we had time and (most importantly) resources, we finally turned to my dream of owning a beach house of our own. This time, the beach would be on Tybee Island, a mile-long barrier island off the coast of Savannah that's only a four-hour drive from our home in Atlanta. After a prolonged hunt—and three unsuccessful bids—we found a two-story concrete-block box, painted in circus shades of blue and yellow. It was stinky and rat-infested, and a squatter had taken up residence, but the price and size were right. It took nearly a year, but eventually we transformed that house into my dream of a throw-back Florida beach cottage painted in a retro turquoise, complete with a hibiscus-pink front door. We furnished it with my basement full of hoarded estate-sale and flea-market finds and christened the house the Breeze Inn, after a fictional motel in my novel *Savannah Breeze*, which was set on Tybee. The very first step in our restoration project was ripping out the old kitchen. In its place, we planned a new galley space, and its centerpiece would be a huge old porcelain farm sink I found at an antique salvage yard.

As soon as we moved into the Breeze, Tom and I started cooking and inviting friends and family to join us around the heart-pine table we'd had crafted from boards taken from our former house in Atlanta. And before long, that big sink became the perfect beach house bathtub for our first grandbaby, Molly. Two years later, after the birth of her little brother, Griffin, our three-bedroom house was feeling mighty cramped when the entire family joined us at the beach. We started searching for something bigger. Eventually, my friend Diane tipped me off that our "forever beach house" was on the market—and the price had recently been slashed.

I toured the house on a cold November day and knew she was right. The house was an original Tybee beach house, circa 1932, and had been owned by the same family for three generations. The location was ideal—one house away from the beach, with ocean views if you craned your neck or stood in the right spot. It had two floors of wrap-around porches, plenty of elbow room, and six bedrooms. Tom was off on a hunting trip out west, so I texted him pictures, and then submitted an offer. We closed on the house the week before Christmas of 2012, and on the day after Christmas, we moved in.

Once again, our first priority was ripping out the funky original kitchen. I found another salvaged farmhouse sink, and our contractors started building new cabinets on-site. This time I named the house Ebbtide, after a fictional beach house I'd created in *Summer Rental*. We bought Ebbtide furnished, but, as usual, I had my own decorating schemes—and yes, another basement-full of hoarded vintage treasures. We sold off most of our inherited furniture but kept the long wooden dining room table and eight sturdy chairs surrounding it, along with an antique oak sideboard. Even before the kitchen was completed, we started cooking and creating new beach house memories. The new stove hadn't been delivered, so I made an old family favorite, pot roast, in an electric skillet, which everybody proclaimed the best pot roast ever.

We roasted oysters on the grill on the downstairs porch, made friends with our new neighbors—one of whom is an amazing gardener, another of whom is as die-hard a fisherman as Tom—and quickly established new traditions in our new old house.

Although we have both beach houses in a vacation rental program and have maintained our full-time home in Atlanta, we spend as much time as possible at the beach. We start each year with a family gathering the week between Christmas and New Year's, hosting a New Year's Eve dinner with tenderloin and shrimp and lots of bubbly, before walking down the boardwalk over the dunes to watch the New Year's Eve fireworks. Our longtime New Year's tradition of an open house in Atlanta has been transferred to Tybee, where we celebrate with Southern good-luck mainstays—collard greens, black-eyed peas, and ham, all fixed with an updated twist. We always roast oysters fresh from the nearby tidal creeks and rivers, and friends arrive with their own covered dishes. In fact, that's basically our modus operandi when we're at the beach. Our menus are fairly simple and ever changing, but we love to cook and entertain together, and do so often. I'm in charge of research and development, finding new recipes, suggesting updates or changes, and usually figuring out where to get the freshest ingredients. Tom is the grill-master and seafood chef. I figure out appetizers, sides, and desserts. He chooses the wine—always white or rosé for me, red for him.

Even if it's just dinner for the two of us, I love to set a pretty table with my basic white outlet store china, augmented with colorful discount-store soup bowls and salad plates and estate-sale table linens, glassware, and serving pieces gathered from my junking forays. Fresh flowers are my favorites, and we've planted herb and flower gardens around Breeze Inn and Ebbtide, but even if I can't find something in bloom, I can always snip some palm fronds or greenery from around the island, or pick up inexpensive cut flowers from nearby supermarkets. From Valentine's Day dinner cooked by the guys to Easter brunch for the family to summer solstice dinners to fireside fall soup suppers for two, we keep it simple and fun, kind of like a day at the beach—any time of year.

The whole point of this book? You can do it, too. You don't have to have an actual beach house to capture that same easygoing atmosphere. The recipes that follow are designed to let you be creative in the kitchen, yet still spend time relaxing with family and guests. Since it's no fun to be chained to a hot stove when everybody else is on the beach or the porch, I suggest you do as we do—delegate! Let one person be the "grill captain" while the prep chefs are slicing tomatoes, peeling shrimp, or shucking corn, and someone else is making the barbecue sauce or throwing dessert together. Although we do have a surprisingly good local island grocery store, our beach house happens to be on a barrier island, ten miles from the nearest big supermarket, and the same is true of many weekend or vacation destinations. So none of these recipes calls for obscure or hard-to-find ingredients, and all can be achieved in even the most sparsely furnished vacation rental. Also, many of my recipes use shortcuts like refrigerated pie crust, box mixes, and frozen foods where appropriate, but most emphasize using fresh, readily available, local ingredients.

The joy of beach house cooking is that it's a lot like my writing process. I start out with an idea of where I want a story to go, but along the way, the plot and characters take on a life of their own. I revise and improvise right up until time to finalize and hit the "send" button on my laptop keyboard. Substitutions, or freestyling, as I like to call it, are encouraged; if you don't have peaches for the cobbler, plums, apricots, or even canned cherry pie filling are just as tasty.

If you didn't save any bleached-out sand dollars or seashells from your last trip to the shore, order online or pick some up at a crafts store. Sprinkle them around your tabletop, interspersed with cheap white candles planted in glass candlesticks or wine goblets from the dollar store. Use inexpensive striped cotton dishtowels as dinner napkins. For a centerpiece, snip some fronds from that potted palm still going strong on your back deck and stick them in a clear glass vase with water. You can even use larger palm fronds as place mats.

Are you starting to feel beachy yet? No? You're gonna need some tunes to put you in the mood. Download anything from my playlist, from the Beach Boys to the Four Tops and Temptations to Bob Marley, or, duh, Jimmy Buffett. Now, uncap a frosty local craft beer, or whomp up a batch of Beergaritas. Put on the Low Country Boil and get out the cocktail sauce, light those candles, slip off your shoes, and open the windows, if only spiritually. *Ahhh.* You're so there.

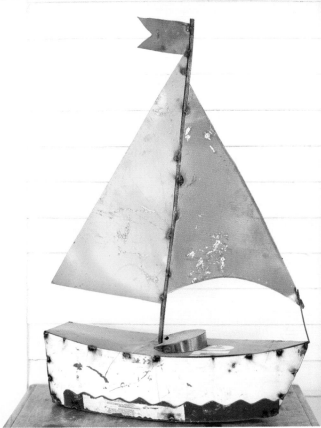

Summer Solstice Dinner

Here in the Deep South, it's usually already plenty steamy by the time the official start of summer rolls around. Even if it's not hot enough to fry an egg on the hood of your car where you live, why not plan to have a lovely, cool dinner that doesn't require firing up the oven in the heat of the day? My tomato pie can be made in the morning, preferably using dead-ripe local tomatoes, and served at room temperature. We usually snag our tomatoes from the garden of our Ebbtide neighbor, Tompkins, but he's probably going to notice if all of y'all do that, so better head to your local produce stand to buy your own 'maters. The chicken salad, one of my most-requested recipes, showed up in Little Bitty Lies, in which the protagonist, Mary Bliss McGowan, fakes her missing husband's death to cash in on his life insurance policy.

SERVES 8

menu

James T's Secret Iced Tea

Zucchini Vichyssoise

Beyond the Grave Chicken Salad

Tomato Pie

Ritualistic Pimento Cheese

Trailer Trash Dessert

James T's Secret Iced Tea

My friend James T. Farmer of Perry, Georgia, is a landscape architect by training and a Southern lifestyle authority by birthright. He is also the author of several beautiful and indispensable gardening, cooking, and entertaining books, including A Time to Celebrate, Dinner on the Grounds, A Time to Cook, *and others. We became fast friends over a shared lunch of fried chicken on the porch at Ebbtide, at which time he revealed the secret of his world-famous iced tea. Two words: Earl Grey. The black leaves in Earl Grey tea have been flavored with the oil of bergamot orange, giving it a lovely, distinctive floral flavor, that in turn elevates James T's iced tea to something very special.*

3 family-size tea bags

1 Earl Grey tea bag

1 cup sugar

Peach wedges, mint sprigs for garnish (optional)

1. Bring 2 cups water to a boil in a saucepan. Add the tea bags, remove from the heat, and let steep for about 5 minutes. Pour the tea into a 1-gallon pitcher, reserving the tea bags in the saucepan.

2. Meanwhile, combine the sugar and 2 cups water in a separate medium saucepan over medium-high heat. Cook just until the sugar dissolves. Remove from the heat, and let stand until cooled.

3. Add the sugar syrup to the tea in the pitcher. Add water to the tea bags in the saucepan. Add to the tea in the pitcher, continuing the process until the mixture measures 1 gallon. Serve over ice, garnished with the peach slices and/or mint sprigs if desired.

Zucchini Vichyssoise

Cold soups, I've learned, are pretty much an acquired taste. I love 'em, but others in my family? Not so much. I love traditional vichyssoise but wanted to change it up a little. I think the addition of zucchini is a happy choice, and the pale green color is divine. Just be sure to use only the pale green and white parts of the leeks to eliminate the possibility of any bitterness. Not a fan of zucchini? Heck, just leave 'em out for a velvety smooth cold soup.

¼ cup (½ stick) unsalted butter

1 Tbsp. olive oil

2 large leeks, white and pale green parts only, thinly sliced

2 cloves garlic, minced

1 ½ lb. Yukon Gold potatoes, peeled and cut into chunks

2 medium zucchini, sliced

4 cups low-sodium chicken broth

1 tsp. kosher salt

½ tsp. freshly ground pepper

½ to 1 cup half-and-half

Chopped chives for garnish

1. Melt the butter and oil in a large stockpot over medium heat. Add the leeks and garlic, and sauté until tender and translucent. Add the potatoes, zucchini, broth, salt, and pepper.

2. Bring to a boil. Reduce the heat and simmer for 30 minutes, or until the potatoes are tender. Let stand for 15 minutes.

3. Puree the soup with an immersion blender or in batches in a blender (be sure to remove the center of the lid to allow steam to escape). Stir in ½ cup half-and-half, adding additional half-and-half, if necessary, to reach the desired consistency. Let cool completely, and refrigerate until ready to serve.

4. Spoon the soup into serving bowls, sprinkle with the chives, and serve.

Beyond the Grave Chicken Salad

The recipe for this divine chicken salad was shared with me after I attended the wake for a dear friend's father. It was the inspiration for the recipe included in Little Bitty Lies, *in which the protagonist mourns the death of her best friend's mother—especially since the mother passed away before revealing the recipe for her heavenly creation. In the book, Mary Bliss imagines the recipe is handed down to her from beyond the grave, hence the name. This has become a staple at baby showers, bridal showers, and yes, funeral receptions.*

For the chicken salad:

1 bunch fresh parsley

1 large onion, quartered

1 tsp. seasoned salt

2 chicken bouillon cubes

5 lb. bone-in chicken breasts

½ cup sour cream

1 Tbsp. honey

For the dressing:

1 cup mayonnaise

½ cup bottled Italian salad dressing

1 Tbsp. distilled white vinegar

1 ½ tsp. celery seed

⅛ tsp. salt

Pinch of paprika

1. Bring 2 quarts water, the parsley, the onion, the seasoned salt, and the bouillon to a boil in a large stockpot. Add the chicken.

2. Reduce the heat and simmer for 30 to 40 minutes or until the chicken is done.

3. Remove the chicken from the water, and let stand until cool enough to handle. Remove the skin and bones. Shred with forks, transfer to a bowl, and refrigerate.

4. Make the dressing by whisking all the ingredients together in a small bowl. Pour 1 cup of the dressing over the shredded chicken. Refrigerate for 1 hour.

5. Combine the remaining dressing with the sour cream and honey. Add the mixture to the chicken, stir to combine, and refrigerate until ready to serve.

Tomato Pie

While preparing a tomato pie as my contribution to a party hosted by my friend Susie, I spied a tub of store-bought pimento cheese in my fridge and decided to try freestyling my recipe. The results were immediate: empty pie pan! The pie is fantastic with my Ritualistic Pimento Cheese, but a good-quality commercial brand like Palmetto is a great stand-in.

4 large ripe tomatoes, thinly sliced

Salt

1 refrigerated pie crust (or frozen deep-dish pie crust)

½ cup mayonnaise

½ cup shredded Parmesan cheese

1 Tbsp. Dijon mustard

¼ cup cooked, crumbled bacon

8 basil leaves, thinly sliced, plus basil leaves for garnish (optional)

¼ tsp. freshly ground pepper

1 cup Ritualistic Pimento Cheese (page 11)

1. Place the tomatoes on several layers of paper towels. Sprinkle generously with the salt, and let stand for about 1 hour. Pat dry.

2. Preheat the oven to 350°F. Unroll the pie crust and fit into a 9-inch deep-dish pie plate. Fold and crimp the edges. (Skip this step if using a frozen crust). Prick the dough with a fork, line with parchment paper, and fill with uncooked beans or rice. Bake for 10 minutes. Remove from the oven, remove the beans or rice and paper, and set aside.

3. In a bowl, stir together the mayonnaise and Parmesan cheese. Brush the mustard all over the baked pie shell.

4. Arrange one-third of the tomato slices on the bottom of the pie crust and sprinkle with half of the bacon, half of the sliced basil, and half of the pepper. Spread the mayonnaise mixture evenly over the tomatoes. Arrange half of the remaining tomato slices over the mayonnaise mixture and sprinkle with the remaining bacon, sliced basil, and pepper. Spread the pimento cheese evenly over the tomatoes, and then arrange the remaining tomato slices on top.

5. Bake for 30 minutes, or until the edges begin to bubble. Let stand for at least 15 minutes before slicing. Garnish with the basil leaves, if desired, and serve.

Ritualistic Pimento Cheese

Being the superstitious type, I have strict rituals I observe when I run away from home to work on my novels. I always burn my favorite red currant aromatherapy candle while writing. I always plot longhand on a yellow legal pad with a fine-tip Sharpie. And I always have the same thing for lunch, which I make at the beginning of the week and then eat every day. Sometimes it's tuna salad. Sometimes it's egg salad. Often, it's this pimento cheese, which I like slathered on thick white bread topped with slices of ripe tomato. I really like to tuck one of these sandwiches wrapped in wax paper in my jacket pocket, as a treat after a beach walk. Be sure to use good-quality Cheddar that you've shredded yourself. The preshredded cheese is coated with a stabilizer, which makes for an inferior sandwich spread.

4 cups shredded extra-sharp Cheddar cheese

1 (7-oz.) jar diced pimentos, drained

⅔ cup mayonnaise (we tested with Duke's)

Juice of 1 lemon

1 Tbsp. Worcestershire sauce

Generous dash of hot sauce

Freshly ground pepper

Place all the ingredients in a bowl and mix well with a fork. Cover and refrigerate for 1 hour before serving.

Trailer Trash Dessert

There are dozens of variations of this recipe on the Internet, but my family refers to this easy ice cream bar dessert as "Trailer Trash" because the ingredients are, well, not exactly gourmet. Still, it's the perfect recipe for a beach house vacation, because even if your summer rental kitchen isn't equipped with a 9-by-13-inch pan, you can always pick up a disposable foil pan when you're buying the rest of the ingredients. And it's so easy, kids can assemble it themselves. Plus, you won't heat up the kitchen! You can usually find the toffee bits in the baking aisle where chocolate chips are sold. If not, buy several candy bars, place them in a zip-top bag, and crush with a rolling pin. (Or a heavy cast-iron skillet!)

24 ice cream sandwiches

1 (11.75-oz.) jar hot fudge topping

1 (12-oz.) jar caramel topping

2 (8-oz.) containers whipped
   topping, thawed

1 (8-oz.) package chocolate-toffee
   bits, divided

1. Unwrap 12 ice cream sandwiches and arrange in a single layer in a 9-by-13-inch baking pan. Using the end of a wooden spoon, poke holes in the ice cream sandwiches.

2. Microwave the hot fudge topping and caramel topping according to the package directions.

3. Drizzle about one-third of the hot fudge topping and caramel topping over the sandwiches, frost with one container of whipped topping, and sprinkle with one-third of toffee bits.

4. Repeat the layers once. Drizzle the remaining hot fudge topping and caramel topping over the whipped topping. Sprinkle with the remaining toffee bits. Cover and freeze until firm. Cut into squares and serve.

Low Country Boil

In late summer and early fall, local shrimp and blue crabs are abundant in the sounds, tidal rivers, and creeks that surround our beach house on Tybee Island, and sweet corn is available, too. Last year, we celebrated our son Andy's thirtieth birthday with a Low Country Boil at Ebbtide, inviting some of his oldest friends to gather to mark his big day. Not everybody adds blue crab to their Low Country Boil, but when the traps we dropped off our friend's dock yielded four dozen specimens in about an hour, they were added to the pot. In addition to the seafood component, it's traditional for the menu to include Savannah red rice, a spicy local specialty, and for an easy green vegetable, fried okra cakes are convenient because they can be made in advance and served at room temperature. A peach and blackberry or blueberry cobbler rounds out a meal that emphasizes local gifts from the garden and the sea. (And a scoop of ice cream on top of warm-from-the-oven cobbler never hurt.)

SERVES 10 TO 12

menu

Low Country Boil

Savannah Red Rice

Fried Okra Cakes

Peach and Berry Cobbler

Low Country Boil

Low Country Boil is a meal—and an event! Here's how it works. You invite some friends over, and you grab the biggest stockpot you can find. If you have one of those nifty outdoor cookers with a propane tank and a stand for your stockpot, that's swell, but a stovetop works well, too. Spread newspapers over your table and put out some nutcrackers and cocktail picks for the blue crabs (if you've been able to procure them), cocktail sauce and lemons for the shrimp, melted butter for the potatoes, plenty of ice-cold beer, and lots of wet naps or paper towels. Here's what you'll need to feed ten to twelve eager pals.

1 (12-oz.) can beer

1 cup Old Bay seasoning

2 lemons, quartered, plus lemon
   wedges for serving

½ cup white wine vinegar

3 lb. medium-size red potatoes,
   unpeeled, halved

4 lb. spicy sausage (such as kielbasa or
   andouille), cut into 2-inch pieces

2 large Vidalia onions, quartered

8 ears corn, shucked and cut in half

1 dozen live blue crabs

3 lb. large shrimp, unpeeled

Cocktail sauce, lemon wedges, melted
   butter (optional) for serving

1. Bring 4 gallons of water, the beer, the Old Bay, the lemon quarters, and the vinegar to a boil in a large stockpot over high heat.

2. Add the potatoes; cook for 5 minutes. Add the sausage and onions. Return to a boil, and cook for 15 minutes. Add the corn; cook for 5 minutes. Add the blue crabs. Return to a boil, and cook for about 6 minutes. Add the shrimp; cook for 4 to 6 minutes, or until the shrimp are pink and the potatoes are tender.

3. Drain the seafood boil in a large colander, and serve with the cocktail sauce, lemon wedges, and melted butter, if desired.

Savannah Red Rice

One of the first friends I made as a newlywed and a newcomer to Savannah was Jacky Blatner Yglesias. Luckily, Jacky likes to go "junking" just as much as I do, so we've spent many happy hours together treasure hunting. Jacky taught me how to head shrimp and how to make red rice, which is a mainstay at the outdoor seafood extravaganza known as a Low Country Boil. Once, we went to jail together in Metter, Georgia, after a late-night car breakdown. But that's a story for another time.

4 slices bacon

½ cup chopped onion

1 (28-oz.) can petite-diced tomatoes, undrained

2 cups white rice

½ cup low-sodium chicken broth

½ tsp. salt

¼ tsp. freshly ground pepper

1. Preheat the oven to 350°F. Grease a 3-quart baking dish and set aside.

2. Cook the bacon in a large skillet over medium-high heat for 6 to 8 minutes, or until crisp. Transfer the bacon to paper towels to drain, reserving the drippings in the skillet. Crumble the bacon.

3. Sauté the onion in the bacon drippings until tender. Add the tomatoes, rice, broth, salt, pepper, and crumbled bacon. Reduce the heat to low and cook for 10 minutes.

4. Pour the mixture into the prepared baking dish, cover with aluminum foil, and bake for 1 hour. Serve warm or at room temperature.

Fried Okra Cakes

When I joined the features staff at the Atlanta Journal-Constitution *in 1983, Thelma's Kitchen on Techwood Avenue was a favored lunchtime destination for cops, AJC reporters, and staff from nearby Grady Memorial Hospital. Thelma's was a soul-food flavored meat-and-three-vegetable luncheonette, and her okra cakes were legendary—especially for me, since I'd never particularly liked the slimy texture of cooked okra before. Thelma's recipe was a closely guarded secret, but I think this version comes pretty close to hitting the key nutty-salty component. Choose small-to-medium tender okra pods and chop them finely by hand, discarding the tough tops and tips. And do use the bacon grease added to the frying oil. About six slices of bacon yields the amount needed for this recipe. I can't prove that using a cast-iron skillet makes a better-tasting okra cake. But it does.*

1 lb. okra, finely chopped

½ cup finely chopped onion

1 large egg, lightly beaten

1 tsp. garlic powder

1 tsp. salt

¼ tsp. freshly ground pepper

½ cup all-purpose flour

½ cup plain cornmeal

1 tsp. baking powder

Canola or peanut oil for frying

¼ cup bacon drippings

1. Place the okra, onion, ½ cup water, egg, garlic powder, salt, and pepper in a large bowl and mix well.

2. Stir the flour, cornmeal, and baking powder together in a separate bowl. Add the flour mixture to the okra mixture and stir until well combined.

3. Heat about 2 inches of oil plus the bacon drippings in a cast-iron or heavy skillet with high sides until the temperature reaches 350°F.

4. Drop the okra batter into the hot oil by heaping tablespoonfuls and cook, in batches, until golden brown, turning once. Drain on paper towels and serve warm.

Peach and Berry Cobbler

For some reason, peaches bought from a roadside farm stand decorated with misspelled, hand-painted signs always taste sweeter to me than the fruit bought at a supermarket. Fruit cobblers and crisps are some of my favorite desserts to make because they are basically a slice, dump, and bake proposition, giving me more time to chillax. Served warm from the oven with a scoop of ice cream, they simply ooze the aroma of tender, homegrown love. And eaten surreptitiously, and cold, the next morning, using the refrigerator door as a shield to hide your transgression from anybody else who might stumble into the kitchen, this cobbler tastes even better.

1 cup granulated sugar, divided

½ cup firmly packed light brown sugar

6 cups peeled and sliced fresh peaches

2 cups blackberries, blueberries, or raspberries

2 tsp. fresh lemon juice

1 tsp. ground cinnamon

¼ tsp. grated nutmeg

Pinch of salt

2 cups milk

2 cups self-rising flour

½ cup (1 stick) salted butter, melted

2 tsp. almond extract

Vanilla ice cream (optional) for serving

1. Preheat the oven to 375°F. Grease a 3-quart baking dish. Combine ½ cup of the granulated sugar and the brown sugar in a small bowl. Combine the peaches, berries, lemon juice, cinnamon, nutmeg, salt, and ½ cup of the sugar mixture in a large bowl, tossing well to coat. Let stand for 30 minutes.

2. Add the remaining ½ cup sugar mixture, if desired, depending on the sweetness of the fruit. Pour into the prepared dish.

3. Stir the milk, flour, melted butter, remaining ½ cup granulated sugar, and almond extract in a medium bowl until well blended. Pour over the fruit mixture and bake, uncovered, for 25 to 30 minutes, or until lightly browned on top. Serve warm with the vanilla ice cream, if desired.

Fourth of July Dinner

Our small town celebrates the Fourth of July in a big way, starting in the morning with a parade of decorated golf carts, baby strollers, riding lawn mowers, and pickup trucks, augmented with the random marching band that doesn't have a better-paying gig someplace else. Around 5 p.m., neighbors drift over to our house with their covered dishes for what we've come to refer to as "Dinner on the Grounds"—a prelude to the big fireworks display down at the lake. Unlike most of our neighbors, we don't picnic at the lake that night. Why? Because Mr. MKA has an irrational hatred of dragging food and equipment several blocks away to be eaten on the ground in a swampy, bug-infested environment. I long ago gave up arguing with him. Most years, my sister-in-law Jeanne and I fire up the skillets and whomp up a mess of fried chicken from her time-tested recipe, and we build our menu around that. True confession: In years when we happen to be at the beach for the Fourth of July and I don't feel like cooking, I call ahead of time and order up boxes of superb fried chicken from the Tybee IGA in my own personal declaration of independence from the tyranny of a hot, greasy kitchen.

SERVES 6 TO 8

menu

Sandbar Sangria

Buttermilk-Brined Fried Chicken

Edna's Potato Salad

Marinated Cucumbers and Onions

Edna's Deviled Eggs

Old Glory Parfaits

Sandbar Sangria

Way back when I was a college kid, sangria was new and exotic—like fondue. And crêpes. Admittedly, I liked sangria better than either of those '70s throwbacks. I prefer it made with my favorite summer sipper, rosé. You can add whatever fruit you like or have on hand. For the fizzy part—you gotta have fizz—I like those flavored sparkling waters, like LaCroix, but you could also double down and use a sparkling wine like prosecco. Be sure to serve it in a clear glass pitcher or decanter, so all can behold the pretty pinkness of your Sandbar Sangria.

2 (750-ml) bottles dry rosé wine, chilled

1 qt. strawberries, hulled and cut in half

2 peaches, peeled and sliced

1 pt. blueberries

1 liter sparkling water, flavored seltzer, or sparkling wine

Place rosé, strawberries, peaches, and blueberries in a bowl and mix well. Cover and refrigerate for 1 hour. Stir in sparkling water before serving.

Buttermilk-Brined Fried Chicken

I thought my late mother's fried chicken was the best I'd ever tasted, until my sister-in-law Jeanne Trocheck came up with this recipe. The secret is letting the chicken pieces soak, preferably overnight, in a bath of buttermilk spiced up with hot sauce. That, plus letting the flour-coated chicken pieces dry out on a raised wire rack before frying, gives you juicy, crispy fried chicken that really will make you want to slap your mama. Another secret is to keep the fried chicken warming in the oven until it's time to serve. Look for a package of cut-up chicken, or buy a 4-pound chicken and cut it up yourself, discarding the backbone and wing tips. If the chicken breasts are overly large, cut them in half crosswise before marinating.

3 cups buttermilk

2 Tbsp. kosher salt

1 Tbsp. hot sauce

2 ½ lb. mixed bone-in chicken pieces

2 cups all-purpose flour

1 cup panko bread crumbs

1 Tbsp. poultry seasoning

½ tsp. paprika

¼ tsp. freshly ground pepper

2 cups vegetable oil for frying

1. Combine the buttermilk, salt, and hot sauce in a large heavy-duty zip-top plastic bag. Add the chicken pieces, seal the bag, and place in a large shallow bowl. Refrigerate at least 4 hours or overnight.

2. Line a large rimmed baking sheet with aluminum foil, and place a wire cooling rack on top.

3. Combine the flour, panko, poultry seasoning, paprika, and pepper in a shallow dish. Remove the chicken from the marinade (discard the marinade). Dredge the chicken pieces thoroughly in the breading mixture, and then place them on the wire rack. Let stand for about 30 minutes, or until the chicken has come to room temperature.

4. Preheat the oven to 300°F. Heat the oil to 350°F in a large cast-iron skillet. Fry the chicken, three or four pieces at a time, for 12 to 15 minutes, turning once. Remove the chicken to a paper towel–lined baking sheet to drain. Place on a clean wire rack set in a rimmed baking sheet, and keep warm in the oven until ready to serve.

Edna's Potato Salad

Ah, potato salad. My grandmother and mother must have made enough of this stuff to feed Pharaoh's army, as my friend Steve would say. I've made my share, too. This is a simple recipe. You can, and I'll admit I've done it, dress it up or down. Omit the hard-boiled eggs and sweet pickle relish and substitute finely chopped bacon, some horseradish, sour cream, and some chopped artichoke hearts. Add dill weed and subtract celery seed. Use tiny, skin-on new potatoes. These are all good, sensible variations, and I don't want to go all potato salad authoritarian on you, but should you do this, you will not have Edna's potato salad. Also? Everybody puts coleslaw on their barbecue. But try a scoop of this stuff, chilled, plopped right on top of your BBQ sammie. You can thank me later.

8 medium Yukon Gold potatoes, unpeeled

8 large eggs, hard-boiled, peeled, and chopped

½ cup finely chopped sweet onion

½ cup finely chopped celery

1 ½ cups mayonnaise

½ cup sweet pickle relish

1 Tbsp. prepared yellow mustard

1 tsp. celery seed

1 tsp. paprika

½ tsp. salt

¼ tsp. freshly ground pepper

1. In a large pot over high heat, bring the potatoes in salted water to cover to a boil. Cook for 15 to 20 minutes, or until the potatoes are tender. Drain and let cool just until able to handle. Peel the potatoes and cut them into cubes.

2. Combine the potatoes, eggs, onion, and celery in a large bowl.

3. Stir the mayonnaise, relish, mustard, celery seed, paprika, salt, and pepper together in a separate bowl. Pour the mayonnaise mixture over the potato mixture and toss well to coat. Cover and refrigerate until ready to serve.

Marinated Cucumbers and Onions

I think my grandmother always had a big recycled pickle jar full of this summer standby in her fridge. It's such an old-timey recipe, I sometimes forget how easy and refreshing these pickles are. For a fun presentation, remove a few vertical strips of cucumber peel before slicing.

2 cucumbers, thinly sliced

1 Vidalia onion, thinly sliced

1 cup apple cider vinegar

½ cup sugar

½ tsp. celery seed

½ tsp. freshly ground pepper

1. Place the cucumbers and onion in a large jar.

2. Bring the vinegar, sugar, and 1 cup water to a boil in a medium saucepan, stirring just until the sugar dissolves. Stir in the celery seed and pepper, and pour over the cucumbers and onion. Seal the jar and refrigerate until time to serve.

Edna's Deviled Eggs

Deviled eggs are basically like a religion in the South. People take this stuff as seriously as they do their King James Bible. My great-grandmother, a dour, mean-spirited old lady we called Dudie, would probably hit you upside the head with her patent leather pocketbook if you tried to top a deviled egg with something as heathen as an anchovy or, Gawd forbid, crème fraîche and caviar. Cook your eggs according to your own conscience and orthodoxy. The following recipe is just a suggestion. Cook as many eggs as you need, and season sparingly, according to your own taste. You do have a deviled egg dish, right? After my mother-in-law, Dot, passed away, we found no fewer than fourteen deviled egg dishes in her kitchen cabinets. And I never knew her to fix deviled eggs.

6 large eggs, hard-boiled and cooled

1 to 2 Tbsp. mayonnaise

2 Tbsp. sweet pickle juice

½ tsp. celery seed

⅛ tsp. dry mustard

Kosher salt and freshly ground
    pepper

Paprika

1. Peel the eggs and cut them in half lengthwise. Scoop out the yolks and place in a bowl. Arrange the whites on a platter.

2. Mash the yolks well with a fork, then add the mayonnaise and pickle juice. Mix with a fork until the desired consistency is reached. Stir in the celery seed, mustard, and salt and pepper to taste. Spoon or pipe the mixture into the egg-white halves. Sprinkle with the paprika and serve.

Old Glory Parfaits

I think parfaits lend themselves perfectly to a Fourth of July celebration—stripes of red, white, and blue coolness, and even easier than pie, right? Which is what you want on a day full of picnics, parades, and fireworks. Make these a day or so ahead and let them chill in the fridge. Or, if you'd prefer, make one large trifle in a cut-glass bowl rather than individual parfaits. Either way—delicious!

1 (4.6-oz.) box cook-and-serve vanilla pudding prepared with 3 cups of milk, according to package directions, and cooled

1 qt. strawberries

1 pt. blueberries

2 cups coarsely crushed vanilla wafers

2 bananas, thinly sliced

1 cup heavy cream

2 Tbsp. powdered sugar

1. Cook the pudding according to the package directions. Let cool. Set aside a few small whole strawberries and blueberries for garnish. Hull and slice the remaining strawberries.

2. Divide half of the pudding among six to eight wine or juice glasses. Top with half of the vanilla wafers and the sliced strawberries. Add the remaining pudding, and then the remaining vanilla wafers, the banana slices, and the blueberries.

3. Beat the cream and powdered sugar at high speed in an electric mixer until stiff peaks form. Top each parfait with the whipped cream and garnish with a halved whole strawberry and a few blueberries. Refrigerate until ready to serve.

Lazy Weekend Brunch

Most weekends at our beach house are busy times. Tom and our son, Andy, are usually setting off early to go fishing, and our daughter, Katie, and son-in-law, Mark, and the grandchildren are headed down to the beach. And if the weather is uncooperative, we always seem to have some ongoing home-improvement project. But occasionally, especially when we have houseguests, we do take time to enjoy a leisurely brunch. This menu is inspired by what's seasonally available to us on Tybee. Although the muffin recipe is inspired by one I found in an old spiral-bound cookbook from a bakery in the Hamptons, blueberries are a huge summer crop in our part of Georgia, as is cantaloupe. The local shrimp and crab used in the quiche are usually plentiful and reasonably priced in the summer.

SERVES 4 TO 6

menu

Prosecco Sippers

Cantaloupe with Lime and Mint

Pig Candy

Blueberry Muffins

Frank's Asparagus and Seafood Quiche

Prosecco Sippers

Bright, bubbly prosecco pairs with your choice (or choices) of fresh fruit for this new twist on the Bellini. I like mine with peaches and a tiny sprig of mint, but maybe you'd prefer strawberries, raspberries, or citrus. If you have guests, make a festive Prosecco Sipper bar and set out several choices of fruit muddles and a small bouquet of fresh herbs including mint, basil, and lemon balm.

½ cup sugar

1 ½ cups chopped fresh fruit (such as stone fruit or citrus sections)

Thinly sliced lemons

Fresh herb sprigs (such as mint, basil, and lemon balm)

Ice

1 (750-ml) bottle prosecco

1. Combine the sugar with ½ cup water in a small saucepan over high heat. Bring to a boil, and cook until the sugar dissolves. Let cool.

2. For each drink, pour about 1 tablespoon of the sugar syrup into an old-fashioned glass, and add the desired amount of chopped fruit. Mash with a muddler or wooden spoon. Add a slice of lemon and an herb sprig, and muddle. Top with the ice cubes and prosecco, and serve.

Cantaloupe with Lime and Mint

In my experience, even the smallest beach grocery store usually sells limes and cantaloupes. And if there's a better-stocked nearby supermarket, you can usually buy fresh mint there. Better yet, grow your own mint at home—just be careful to plant it in a pot in the ground because it's wildly invasive. But even without the mint, this is an easy, fresh-tasting breakfast addition. If you're feeling fancy, scoop the melon into balls.

1 cantaloupe, peeled, seeded, and cut into cubes

1 tsp. grated lime zest plus 3 Tbsp. juice (2 limes)

2 Tbsp. chopped fresh mint

1 tsp. honey

¼ tsp. kosher salt

Place the cantaloupe in a bowl. Stir the lime zest and juice, mint, honey and salt in a separate bowl. Pour over the cantaloupe and toss well to coat. Cover and refrigerate until ready to serve.

Pig Candy

Pig candy, or brown sugar–spiced bacon, has dozens of variations, most of which you can find on the Internet. You could add extra heat, with Cajun seasoning, or make it extra sweet, with cinnamon or even a basting of maple syrup. Let's face it, there's no WRONG way to make this stuff—unless you burn it, or bake it flat on a pan, which guarantees you a nasty mess, not that I would know anything about such a thing. Oh no. That would be very, very wrong.

¾ cup firmly packed dark brown sugar

1 ½ tsp. dry mustard

¾ tsp. cayenne pepper

1 lb. thick-cut bacon

1. Preheat the oven to 350°F. Line two rimmed baking sheets with aluminum foil and top each with an oven-safe baking rack.

2. Combine the brown sugar, mustard, and cayenne pepper in a large zip-top plastic bag. Place the bacon, two or three strips at a time, in the bag, and shake to coat.

3. Transfer the bacon to the wire racks and pat with any leftover sugar mixture. Bake for 30 to 40 minutes, or until the bacon is cooked through. Remove the bacon to parchment paper to cool, and serve.

Blueberry Muffins

The birds always beat me to the berries in my Atlanta backyard, but since blueberries are such a big crop in Georgia, it's not hard to find commercially grown ones. These muffins, inspired by a recipe from a now-defunct bakery in Southampton, New York, are so moist, they need no additional butter or jam topping.

3 cups all-purpose flour

1 ¼ cups granulated sugar

4 ½ tsp. baking powder

½ tsp. baking soda

½ tsp. salt

2 cups blueberries

1 ¼ cups milk

1 cup (2 sticks) unsalted butter, melted

2 large eggs, beaten

1 Tbsp. grated lemon zest

1 tsp. vanilla extract

2 Tbsp. turbinado sugar (optional)

1. Preheat the oven to 400°F. Line 18 muffin cups with paper liners.

2. Combine the flour, granulated sugar, baking powder, baking soda, and salt in a large bowl. Add the blueberries, and toss gently to coat.

3. Whisk the milk, melted butter, eggs, lemon zest, and vanilla extract together in a separate bowl. Add to the flour mixture and stir gently just until combined.

4. Spoon the batter into the muffin cups with an ice cream scoop. Sprinkle with the turbinado sugar if desired. Bake for 22 to 25 minutes, or until the muffins are browned and a wooden pick inserted in the center comes out clean. Remove the muffins from the pan, and let cool on wire racks before serving.

Frank's Asparagus and Seafood Quiche

This quiche came from one of my oldest, dearest friends in the world, Sue Boore Foster. Sue's father, Frank Boore, was the longtime owner of two beloved St. Petersburg restaurants, Aunt Hattie's and Uncle Ed's. When Sue offered her dad's seafood quiche recipe, all I could say was "yes, please!" I did substitute crabmeat for the ½ cup of scallops Frank specified, because crab is more readily available where we live, but if you have access to scallops, go for it! If you end up buying a 1-pound container of picked fresh crabmeat from the seafood market, save any leftovers for the Crab Cakes with Mango Salsa recipe found on page 109.

1 refrigerated pie crust (or frozen deep-dish pie crust)

1 ½ cups chopped cooked peeled shrimp

1 cup shredded sharp Cheddar cheese

1 cup (2- to 3-inch pieces) asparagus

½ cup crabmeat (backfin is fine), picked over

1 ½ cups half-and-half

3 extra-large or jumbo eggs, lightly beaten

½ tsp. salt

½ tsp. freshly ground pepper

½ tsp. garlic powder

¼ tsp. dried dill weed

1. Preheat the oven to 350°F. Unroll the pie crust and fit it into a deep-dish pie plate. Fold and crimp the edges. (Skip this step if using a frozen crust.) Line the crust with parchment paper and fill with uncooked beans or rice. Bake for 10 minutes, then remove from the oven, remove the beans or rice and paper, and set aside.

2. Sprinkle the crust with the shrimp, cheese, asparagus, and crabmeat.

3. In a bowl, whisk the half-and-half, eggs, salt, pepper, garlic powder, and dill together; pour over the filling. Bake for 40 minutes, or until the quiche is set. Serve warm or at room temperature.

Beach Picnic

The perfectly warm days of late spring or early fall never fail to lure us out to the beach, or sometimes onto the boat we keep at a nearby marina. Somehow, I manage to overcome Tom's resistance to dining al fresco by promising him that ALL the prep will be done in advance, in our kitchen. And then I enlist the boys, i.e., Andy and son-in-law Mark, to load up the beach cart with the cooler, blankets, and picnic baskets. Designing an easy, interesting menu of mostly finger foods is another way to guarantee a fun picnic. I pack frozen bottles of water along with the cold drinks to keep everything properly chilled and a baggie of hand wipes for après picnic cleanup. Beachy Ceviche is a new but welcome addition to the picnic lineup. And the peach mustard for the Havarti and ham sandwiches is an oh-so-easy condiment you'll want to make again to dress up grilled chicken or pork tenderloin. Presliced watermelon wedges sprinkled with a little sea salt are a refreshing palate cleanser. But the item everybody seems most interested in is dessert, and these sweet and nutty butterscotch brownies are the perfect bribe to enlist help to carry the picnic gear back home.

SERVES 6

menu

Beachy Ceviche

Ham and Havarti Sandwiches with
Peach-Mustard Spread

Butterscotch Brownies

watermelon wedges

Beachy Ceviche

The only way I could get Tom to agree to a trip to Hawaii last summer was to promise him we'd all go charter fishing on Maui. Accompanied by old, dear friends BJ and Micki, we set out from Lahaina Harbor aboard the Luckey Strike *for a most memorable trip. As the sun rose, we saw Molokai and Lanai rising through the mist. And then the mate shouted, "fish on!" It was the beginning of an unforgettable day, as the four of us caught the Hawaiian versions of wahoo and tuna. During the return trip to the dock, the mate handed around chunks of the just-cleaned catch with packets of pink Hawaiian sea salt for our first samples of seaside sushi. On the way back to our rented condo, we picked up local limes, our own Hawaiian salt, cilantro, red bell peppers, and a jalapeño pepper, and fixed what inspired this ceviche. One caution: With ceviche, the acid in the lime juice "cooks" the fish, which must be absolutely fresh. Don't attempt this recipe unless you've caught the fish yourself, you see it coming off the fishing boats at the dock, or you have absolute trust in your seafood market.*

2 large limes

1 lb. very fresh semi-firm skinless white fish fillets (such as grouper, sea bass, trout, or flounder), cut into small pieces

1 tomato, chopped

1 small red bell pepper, chopped

1 jalapeño chile, seeded and minced

½ cup chopped fresh cilantro

1 tsp. sea salt

Tortilla chips for serving

Squeeze the juice from the limes, and pour into a medium bowl. Add the fish, tomato, bell pepper, jalapeño, cilantro, and salt. Cover and refrigerate for at least 1 hour. Serve cold with tortilla chips.

Ham and Havarti Sandwiches with Peach-Mustard Spread

I think a beach picnic, even a picnic with "just" sandwiches, should be more memorable—and delicious—than everyday picnic fare, especially since boneless ready-to-serve hams are so readily available. Purchase deli-sliced Havarti and brioche or batards for the sandwich bread. The Peach-Mustard Spread makes 2 cups. You can refrigerate leftovers for up to two weeks.

For the sandwiches:
1 boneless sliced heat-and-serve ham quarter
2 large navel oranges
1 (12-oz.) can cola
½ cup firmly packed dark brown sugar
1 tsp. ground cloves

6 French or crusty bread rolls, halved horizontally
1 lb. sliced Havarti cheese
1 (5-oz.) package baby arugula

For the peach-mustard spread:
1 cup peach preserves
1 cup grainy mustard

1. Preheat the oven to 325°F. Place the ham in a baking dish.

2. Slice 1 orange and place the slices between the ham slices and over the ham.

3. Grate the zest and squeeze the juice from the remaining orange into a bowl and add the cola, brown sugar, and cloves. Pour over the ham. Bake for 30 to 35 minutes, or until the ham is browned. Let cool.

4. To make the spread, stir the preserves and mustard together in a small bowl. Spoon a little onto the cut sides of each roll. Top evenly with ham slices, cheese slices, and arugula. Serve.

Butterscotch Brownies

These may be the ultimate salty-sweet lunchbox-type treat and, as a bonus, they are a one-bowl, one-pan trick pony.

1 cup firmly packed light brown sugar

½ cup (1 stick) salted butter, melted

1 large egg, beaten

1 ½ tsp. bourbon or vanilla extract

1 cup all-purpose flour

1 tsp. kosher salt

¾ tsp. baking powder

1 cup chopped pecans, toasted

1 cup butterscotch baking chips

1. Preheat the oven to 350°F. Line an 8-inch square baking pan with aluminum foil, allowing 2 to 3 inches to extend over the sides of the pan.

2. Combine the brown sugar, melted butter, egg, and bourbon in a large bowl. Stir in the flour, salt, and baking powder. Stir in the pecans and butterscotch chips.

3. Pour the batter into the prepared pan and bake for 25 minutes, or until the center is set. Let cool in the pan for 30 minutes. Using the foil sides as handles, remove the brownies from the pan, and let cool completely on a wire rack. Cut into squares and serve.

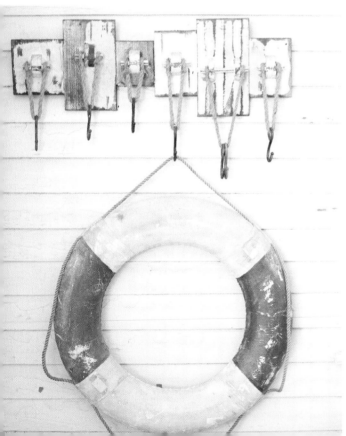

Book Bash Cocktail Party

As an author myself, I love to help friends celebrate the publication of a new book. And when those friends happen to include cookbook authors like fellow Savannah residents Martha Giddens Nesbit and Johnathon Barrett, you know the food had better be fabulous. I've included my versions of some of John and Martha's recipes here, and added a couple of cocktail party standbys of my own. A word to the wise: In our small beach community, a cocktail party is more like a stand-up buffet, consisting of heavy appetizers, albeit mostly ones that don't require a fork, and LOTS of good bourbon, which Tom insists upon. We also usually create a signature cocktail to tie in with the party.

SERVES 12 TO 14

menu

Tybee Tea Cocktail

Marinated Shrimp

Savannah Spinach Squares

Smoked Trout Dip

Baked Crab and Artichoke Dip

Marinated Beef Tenderloin with Fig-Onion Jam

Lemon Bars

Dark Chocolate–Dipped Cheesecake Bites

Tybee Tea Cocktail

I've seen versions of this delicious cross between a mint julep and an Arnold Palmer called the Country Boy, Tipsy Arnold Palmer, and even Lil' Ass Kicker. When we joined several other couples to throw an engagement party hoedown for our dear friend's daughter, we made our own version and called it Tennessee Tea in honor of the happy couple's new home. The result? The millennial crowd stampeded to get at it. Here's my own version, made with James T's iced tea, store-bought lemonade, and a mint simple syrup. I call it Tybee Tea. You'll call for another round!

1 large bunch fresh mint, divided

1 cup sugar

2 qt. James T's Secret Iced Tea (page 3)

2 qt. lemonade

Bourbon

Lemon slices for serving

1. Wash the mint. Coarsely chop enough mint (including stems) to equal 1 cup. Set aside the remaining mint for garnish.

2. Combine the sugar and 1 cup water in a small saucepan. Bring to a boil and cook until the sugar dissolves. Remove from the heat, add the chopped mint, cover, and let steep for 1 hour. Pour through a fine wire-mesh sieve into a clean jar or bowl, and discard the mint.

3. Combine the iced tea and lemonade in a large pitcher, punch bowl, or glass drink dispenser. For each drink, fill an old-fashioned glass with ice, add some of the tea mixture, stir in 1 teaspoon mint syrup and a splash of the bourbon, and garnish with the reserved mint and a lemon slice. Serve.

Marinated Shrimp

We've served this lime juice and cilantro–based shrimp recipe at all kinds of gatherings and in all kinds of ways: over chopped romaine lettuce as a first-course salad, in fancy little glass bowls at dinner parties, and my favorite way, heaped in a giant clamshell and accompanied by cocktail picks. Just don't leave the shrimp in the acidic marinade for more than eight hours, or it will get tough and rubbery.

3 lb. large shrimp, unpeeled

1 large lemon, quartered

2 Tbsp. Old Bay seasoning

2 Tbsp. grated lime zest plus ¾ cup juice (6 limes)

½ cup red wine vinegar

¼ cup sugar

1 ½ Tbsp. Dijon mustard

4 cloves garlic

1 ½ tsp. crushed red pepper

½ tsp. salt

¾ cup vegetable oil

½ cup chopped fresh cilantro

1 red onion, thinly sliced

1 yellow onion, thinly sliced

1 red bell pepper, thinly sliced

1. Bring 3 quarts water to a boil in a large stockpot. Add the shrimp, lemon, and Old Bay. Cook for 3 minutes, or until the shrimp just turn pink and their tails begin to curl. Drain and rinse with cold water. Peel the shrimp and devein, if desired.

2. Combine the lime zest and juice, vinegar, sugar, mustard, garlic, crushed red pepper, and salt in a blender or food processor; blend for 30 seconds. Add the oil in a slow, steady stream, and blend until combined. Blend in the cilantro.

3. Combine the marinade, cooked shrimp, onions, and bell pepper in a large zip-top plastic bag. Seal the bag, and refrigerate for 6 to 8 hours.

4. Remove the shrimp from the marinade, and serve with toothpicks or over greens.

Savannah Spinach Squares

I met Savannah cooks and hosts extraordinaire Tom White and Johnathon Scott Barrett in 1999, when I was writing Savannah Blues. *I was invited to a dinner given by members of their supper club and was overwhelmed by the warmth of their hospitality—and the excellence of their food and drinks. They subsequently hosted a fabulous book party to honor me at their beautiful home in Ardsley Park, and I returned the favor some years later when John's cooking memoir,* Rise and Shine, *was published. These spinach squares are just the thing for your own buffet, but you really must use fresh spinach, not frozen.*

3 Tbsp. olive oil

2 Tbsp. minced garlic

1 lb. baby spinach, chopped

1 (15-oz.) container ricotta

1 (8-oz.) package shredded Italian blend cheese

3 large eggs, lightly beaten

6 Tbsp. (¾ stick) salted butter, melted

⅔ cup self-rising flour

1 tsp. salt

¼ tsp. freshly ground pepper

¼ tsp. grated nutmeg

1 pint cherry or grape tomatoes

Wooden cocktail skewers

1. Preheat the oven to 350°F. Butter or lightly grease a 9-by-13-inch baking dish and set aside.

2. Heat the oil in a large skillet over medium heat. Add the garlic and cook for about 30 seconds, just until fragrant. Stir in the spinach; cover and cook until the spinach wilts. Uncover and cook 3 to 4 minutes longer. Transfer the spinach to a colander to drain, pressing with a paper towel to remove as much liquid as possible.

3. Combine the ricotta, Italian blend cheese, eggs, and melted butter in a large bowl. Add the spinach, and stir until combined. Stir in the flour, salt, pepper, and nutmeg. Pour into the prepared baking dish, and spread into an even layer with a spatula. Bake for about 40 minutes, or until the top begins to brown and the casserole is set. Let cool completely.

4. Cut into 1-inch squares. Top each square with a tomato and pierce with a cocktail skewer. Serve.

Smoked Trout Dip

No visit to the Gulf beaches near my hometown of St. Pete is complete without a stop at Ted Peters Famous Smoked Fish, which has been serving its famous smoked mullet and mackerel since 1951. Tom decided to come up with his own smoked fish dip after an especially successful day of fishing for rainbow and brown trout on the Chattahoochee River outside Atlanta. Before he fires up our smoker, Tom soaks the trout for about one hour in a saltwater brine, using ½ cup kosher salt and enough water to cover the fish. He cooks the fish on a rack in the smoker at a temperature between 240°F and 260°F for around two hours, less if the trout are small, being careful not to let the trout dry out. If you don't have an angler in the family, buy trout at a trusted seafood market and smoke according to your smoker's instructions. Or check to see if your local seafood market sells it already smoked.

8 oz. smoked trout, skinned, deboned, and coarsely chopped

1 cup mayonnaise

½ cup minced sweet onion

2 Tbsp. prepared horseradish

2 Tbsp. chopped fresh chives

1 Tbsp. chopped fresh dill, plus extra for garnish

1 Tbsp. fresh lemon juice

1 Tbsp. capers

Celery sticks, carrot sticks, red bell pepper strips, crackers (optional) for serving

Gently stir the trout, mayonnaise, onion, horseradish, chives, dill, lemon juice, and capers in a bowl until combined. Cover and refrigerate until ready to serve. Garnish with the dill and serve with the celery sticks, carrot sticks, red bell pepper strips, and crackers, if desired.

Baked Crab and Artichoke Dip

The tidal creeks in and around our home on Tybee Island are home to the variety of Atlantic blue crab whose name, Callinectes sapidus, *comes from the Greek for "beautiful swimmer" and Latin for "savory." Happy are the days we spend with Molly and Griffin, who love netting their beautiful swimmers as much as we do preparing and serving this hot crab dip. Five-year-old Griff especially loves wielding the little wooden mallets used to crack the cooked claws. Sometimes, for a change of pace, I sauté 3 ½ cups baby kale leaves in 2 tablespoons of olive oil, drain in a colander, and add to the dip before baking.*

8 oz. cream cheese, softened

1 cup mayonnaise

2 Tbsp. Dijon mustard

1 Tbsp. olive oil

1 cup diced sweet onion

2 cloves garlic, minced

2 (14-oz.) cans artichoke hearts,
    drained and coarsely chopped

2 Tbsp. Old Bay seasoning

1 Tbsp. dry sherry

2 cups freshly grated Parmesan
    cheese, divided

1 lb. claw crabmeat, picked over

1 baguette, thinly sliced and toasted,
    for serving

1. Preheat the oven to 350°F. Grease a 9-by-13-inch baking dish or two 2-quart baking dishes. Beat the cream cheese, mayonnaise, and mustard in a large bowl with an electric mixer until smooth. Set aside.

2. Heat the oil in a large skillet over medium heat and add the onion. Cook for 3 to 4 minutes, or until tender. Add the garlic and cook for 1 minute longer. Add the onion-garlic mixture to the cream cheese mixture.

3. Drain the artichoke hearts in a colander, and press down gently with paper towels to remove additional liquid. Add to the cream cheese mixture. Stir in the Old Bay, sherry, and 1 ½ cups of the Parmesan. Fold in the crabmeat.

4. Spoon the mixture into the prepared baking dish and sprinkle the remaining Parmesan on top. Bake for about 30 minutes, or until the top is lightly browned and the edges are bubbly. Serve with the toasted baguette slices.

Marinated Beef Tenderloin with Fig-Onion Jam

Nothing seems quite as elegant—and yet is so deceptively easy to cook—as a beef tenderloin. My friend Jeanie Payne gifted me with a copy of American Pi, *a fund-raiser cookbook published by Atlanta's Paideia School, from which all three of her children graduated. Jeanie helped test many of the recipes in the cookbook, and after she served a version of this tenderloin at one dinner party, all her guests voted it Most Likely to Succeed. Tom has adapted the recipe to fit his tastes and methods. Being an engineer, he is a firm believer in always using a meat thermometer, and it pains me to admit it, but he's right (this time).*

1 (5- to 6-lb.) beef tenderloin, trimmed

3 cups dry white wine

2 cups low-sodium soy sauce

1 cup Worcestershire sauce

1 cup canola oil

Juice of 2 lemons

2 Tbsp. Dijon mustard

6 cloves garlic, minced

2 Tbsp. sea salt

1 Tbsp. peppercorns

3 to 4 dozen crusty dinner rolls for serving

1 recipe Fig-Onion Jam (recipe follows) for serving

1. Place the tenderloin in a large glass baking dish or plastic container.

2. Combine the wine, soy sauce, Worcestershire sauce, oil, lemon juice, mustard, garlic, salt, and peppercorns in a large liquid measuring cup. Pour over the tenderloin and turn to coat all sides. Cover and refrigerate for at least 8 hours, turning occasionally.

3. Preheat the oven to 350°F. Transfer the tenderloin to a baking pan and discard the marinade.

4. Bake the beef about 40 to 45 minutes or until a meat thermometer registers 135°F. Tent loosely with foil and let rest for 20 minutes. (The temperature will rise to 145°F, for medium-rare.)

5. Slice the beef and serve on dinner rolls with the Fig-Onion Jam.

Fig-Onion Jam

Our Atlanta home has a veritable grove of fig trees, but last year was the first year the birds decided to share the fruit. Naturally, I had to come up with new and delicious ways to use all those sweet, luscious figs. A savory jam, which could be used on sandwiches or alongside meats, seemed to be the way to go. Our figs are the Brown Turkey variety, but you can substitute whatever variety grows near you. If your figs are very ripe, you may want to cut back on the sugar.

¼ cup olive oil

1 sweet onion, thinly sliced

2 cups ripe figs

2 Tbsp. sugar

1 tsp. chopped fresh rosemary

¼ cup balsamic vinegar

1 tsp. freshly ground pepper

Salt

1. Heat the oil in a heavy skillet over medium-low heat. Add the onion and cook for 15 to 20 minutes, stirring occasionally, until lightly browned and caramelized.

2. Add the figs, sugar, and rosemary. Cook for 10 minutes, stirring constantly with a wooden spoon and using the back of the spoon to mash the figs as they soften.

3. Add the vinegar and pepper. Season with salt to taste. Transfer to a jar or container with a lid and refrigerate until ready to serve. Store jam in the refrigerator for up to two weeks.

Lemon Bars

I love anything lemon flavored, and these bars—my riff on those from Kathleen's Bake Shop Cookbook—*are both sweet and tart. Do make sure and let them cool completely before cutting; otherwise, you'll have a gooey (but delicious) mess.*

¾ cup (1 ½ sticks) salted butter, softened

2 ⅓ cups granulated sugar, divided

1 ½ cups plus 5 Tbsp. all-purpose flour, divided

½ cup finely chopped slivered almonds

1 tsp. grated lemon zest plus ¾ cup juice (4 lemons), divided

4 large eggs, at room temperature

Powdered sugar

1. Preheat the oven to 350°F. Beat the butter, ⅓ cup of the granulated sugar, 1½ cups of the flour, the almonds, and the lemon zest with an electric mixer until a stiff dough forms. Press the dough into the bottom of an ungreased 9-by-13-inch baking pan. Bake for 20 minutes, or until the crust is lightly browned and set. Remove from the oven.

2. Meanwhile, lightly whisk the eggs in a large bowl. Combine the remaining 2 cups granulated sugar and the 5 tablespoons flour in a separate bowl. Gradually stir the sugar mixture into the eggs. Stir in the lemon juice and immediately pour over the hot crust. Bake for 20 minutes, or until the lemon layer is firm to the touch. Let cool completely in the pan on a wire rack. Cut into bars, dust with powdered sugar, and serve.

Dark Chocolate-Dipped Cheesecake Bites

If you're just going to have a dessert nibble, I think it should be a nibble so decadent and rich that it'll send you directly to sugar nirvana. This ought to do it. I used Ghirardelli dark melting wafers, but bittersweet chocolate chips could also work, thinned with a little melted shortening.

2 cups crushed gingersnaps (about 42 cookies)

6 Tbsp. (¾ stick) unsalted butter, melted

1 lb. cream cheese, softened

¾ cup sugar

2 Tbsp. cornstarch

⅛ tsp. sea salt or kosher salt

2 large eggs

2 Tbsp. fresh lemon juice

1 (10-oz.) package dark chocolate melting wafers

Coarse sea salt for sprinkling

1. Preheat the oven to 325°F. Line an 8-inch square baking pan with aluminum foil, allowing 2 to 3 inches to extend over the sides of the pan.

2. Mix the crushed gingersnaps with the melted butter. Pat the crumb mixture into the bottom of the prepared baking pan.

3. Beat the cream cheese, sugar, cornstarch, and salt with an electric mixer until smooth. Add the eggs, one at a time, beating just until incorporated. Beat in the lemon juice.

4. Pour the cream cheese mixture over the crust and bake for about 30 minutes, or until set. Turn off the oven and leave the cheesecake in the oven for 20 minutes, then remove and let cool. Cover and freeze for up to 2 hours.

5. Remove the cheesecake from the pan using the aluminum foil as handles, and cut into 1-inch cubes.

6. Place the chocolate in a bowl and microwave according to the package directions. Spoon a small amount of the melted chocolate over each cheesecake bite, allowing it to drip over the sides of the pan. Immediately sprinkle the tops with coarse sea salt. Refrigerate until ready to serve.

After a Day at the Beach

I think this simple menu is a great change-up when you're convinced you can't stare another grilled hamburger or baked bean in the face. Depending on your mood, choose the light and simple Fresh Tomato Pasta—a favorite of mine to make when I'm holed up at the beach house, writing. Or go for the main-dish salad instead. Growing up near the large Greek community of Tarpon Springs, Florida, I've always loved Mediterranean cuisine. Louis Pappas was probably the best-known local Greek restaurant, and for years you could buy a prepared version of their Greek salad in the deli department at Publix, another Florida-based institution. I'd thought the recipe was gone with the ages because Pappas closed many years ago. Imagine my joy when my late mother-in-law, Dot, gifted me with a yard-sale copy of the Junior League of Tampa's Gasparilla Cookbook *containing the treasured Louis Pappas salad recipe. For dessert, lemon granita–filled lemons sound fancier than they actually are, but if you're really feeling like a slacker, you can easily fake it with some store-bought gelato popped into hollowed-out lemons, and they'll still call you Martha Junior.*

SERVES 4

menu

Fresh Tomato Pasta

Grilled Garlic Bread

Greek Salad My Way

Frozen Lemon Granita

Fresh Tomato Pasta

Twice a year, I go on a writing retreat with my author pals Margaret Maron, Bren Witchger, Diane Chamberlain, Katy Munger, Alex Sokoloff, and Sarah Shaber. We run away from home with our laptops and yellow legal pads and burrow in for five days to write, brainstorm, write some more, and offer each other encouragement and advice, stopping only for very simple meals—and more brainstorming. Because our retreat house kitchen is rudimentary (okay, positively primitive), our meals have to be easy to prepare—and delicious. We all take turns preparing dinner. Usually I bring a beef stew, or chili, or sometimes roast a chicken. But one year, the retreat was in August for the first time, and the last thing we all wanted was something heavy. Luckily, before heading over to the retreat house, I had taken a leisurely drive around the countryside and stumbled across a nearby peach orchard. I bought two sacks of sweet, juicy Georgia Belle peaches, some corn, and blueberries, all grown on or near the property. The peach man directed me to another produce stand just up the road, where I scored some fabulous locally grown tomatoes, the star of this easy-peasy dish.

1 lb. linguine	2 cups baby arugula
Salt and freshly ground pepper	1 small red onion, halved and thinly
2 ½ lb. tomatoes	sliced
3 Tbsp. extra-virgin olive oil	1 (6-oz.) container shaved Parmesan
2 Tbsp. red wine vinegar	cheese, divided

1. Bring a large pot of salted water to a boil. Add the linguine and cook according to the package directions.

2. Meanwhile, chop the tomatoes into ½-inch pieces and put them, along with their juices, in a large bowl. Add the oil and vinegar, and season with the salt and pepper to taste.

3. Add the arugula and onion to the tomatoes. Drain the pasta and pour over the vegetables. Let stand for 2 minutes, and then toss until the pasta is coated. Stir in half of the cheese. Season with additional salt and pepper to taste. Serve with the remaining cheese.

Grilled Garlic Bread

This simple preparation makes outstanding garlic bread, but if you don't feel like firing up the grill outside, simply use a stovetop grill pan.

¼ cup (½ stick) unsalted butter, softened

2 Tbsp. freshly grated Parmesan cheese

2 Tbsp. chopped fresh parsley

1 large clove garlic, minced

1 loaf crusty French or Italian bread, halved lengthwise

1. Preheat a charcoal or gas grill to medium-high heat. Combine the butter, cheese, parsley, and garlic in a small bowl. Spread the butter mixture on the cut sides of the bread.

2. Grill the bread for 1 to 2 minutes on each side. Wrap in foil, and keep warm until ready to serve.

Greek Salad My Way

Whenever we make this salad, Tom wonders why it doesn't have meat. So, I thought, why not give the man what he wants? Earlier in the day, marinate the steak in some of the dressing, if you'd like, and either grill it ahead of time or just before serving. Most authentic Greek salad recipes call for anchovies, which he loves, but I don't. So I serve the anchovies in a little dish on the side. His side. Far away from my side.

For the potato salad:

6 medium Yukon Gold potatoes

2 Tbsp. red wine vinegar

Salt

½ cup mayonnaise

¼ cup chopped fresh parsley

½ cup thinly sliced green onions

For the steak:

½ cup olive oil

½ cup distilled white vinegar

1 tsp. dried oregano

Salt and freshly ground pepper

12 oz. sirloin steak

For the Greek salad:

1 large head Romaine lettuce, coarsely chopped

1 lb. shrimp, cooked and peeled

2 large tomatoes, cut into wedges

1 cucumber, peeled and cut into spears

4 radishes, thinly sliced

1 avocado, pitted and sliced

7 oz. feta cheese, coarsely crumbled

1 green bell pepper, cut into rings

12 pepperoncini

12 Greek olives

6–8 anchovy fillets

1. *Make the potato salad:* Bring the potatoes in salted water to cover to a boil. Cook for 15 to 20 minutes, or until the potatoes are tender. Drain and let cool just until able to handle. Peel the potatoes and cut into cubes. Place in a bowl and sprinkle with the vinegar and a pinch of the salt. In a separate bowl, combine the mayonnaise, parsley, and green onions. Add to the potato mixture and stir well to coat; season with additional salt to taste.

2. *Make the steak:* Whisk together the oil, vinegar, oregano, and salt and pepper to taste. Rub the steak with 2 teaspoons of the dressing, and let marinate for up to two hours. Set the remaining dressing aside.

3. Heat a grill pan over medium-high heat. Cook the steak for 3 to 4 minutes on each side, or to the desired doneness. Let rest for 5 to 10 minutes; cut into thin slices against the grain.

4. *Make the salad:* Arrange all the ingredients on a large platter. Serve.

Frozen Lemon Granita

I first served this recipe years ago at the end of a progressive neighborhood dinner party. After heavy appetizers and hearty entrées (and lots of wine), my guests were wowed by this simple-to-make but impressive-looking dessert. You could dress it up with some store-bought almond cookies served on the side, or with a drizzle of blueberry puree, but honestly, this is one lily that needs no gilding.

6 large lemons

1 cup sugar

2 Tbsp. citrus-flavored vodka or
    limoncello

Fresh mint sprigs for serving
    (optional)

1. Cut a small slice from one end of each lemon to create a stable base. Cut ¼ to ½ inch from the other end. Using a paring knife or small serrated knife, carefully cut around the pith, making sure not to cut through the bottom of the lemon.

2. Scoop out the lemon flesh with a spoon into a bowl. Squeeze all of the scooped-out lemons—you should have 1 ¼ to 1 ½ cups juice.

3. Bring 3 cups water and the sugar to a boil in a medium saucepan, and cook until the sugar is dissolved. Remove from the heat and whisk in 1 cup of the lemon juice. Stir in additional juice, 1/4 cup at a time, adding more according to taste. Stir in the vodka and pour into a shallow glass or metal baking dish. Freeze for 1 hour.

4. Remove the dish from the freezer and scrape the ice crystals with a fork; return to the freezer. Repeat the process every hour for 2 to 3 hours, or until the granita is frozen and fluffy.

5. Scoop the granita into the lemon shells, garnish with mint, if desired, and serve immediately.

Catch of the Day

My husband and son are SERIOUS fishermen who've been known to venture out in their boat in all kinds of weather conditions. They rarely come back empty-handed, but when that does happen, we usually have some of their catch from another day, filleted and frozen in fresh water, in heavy-duty freezer bags. Tom came up with the idea of making fish "bites" when we were invited to a covered-dish supper at the home of a friend on Tybee, and they are wonderful served up in taco form. As for the side dishes, we're lucky to count some amazing chef/gardeners among our circle of close friends. Linda Christian farms in south Georgia, but always jumps at the chance to join us on Tybee—and she gets invited often because she always arrives with a cooler of just-picked produce, which she usually proceeds to cook up for an appreciative audience.

SERVES 6

menu

Tybee Fish Tacos

Vinegar Slaw

Corn Fritters with Hot 'n' Sweet Dipping Sauce

Old School Mac 'n' Cheese

Frozen Key Lime Pie Pops

Tybee Fish Tacos

When we were remodeling Ebbtide a few years ago, our painter, Roz, came down from Atlanta to stay with us while she painted the kitchen cabinets, since they were being built on-site. As part of her pay, every day we would bring her fish tacos from a different restaurant on Tybee. Eventually, Tom came up with a recipe using his own fresh-caught flounder, which she declared easily equal to even the best takeout.

2 ½ to 3 lb. firm white fish fillets (such as flounder, redfish, trout, or mahi-mahi)

2 cups panko bread crumbs

2 Tbsp. Cajun seasoning

2 large eggs, lightly beaten

1 cup half-and-half

Hot sauce, divided

¾ cup plain Greek yogurt

1 large avocado, halved, pitted, and peeled

Juice of 2 limes

2 Tbsp. chopped fresh cilantro

Canola oil for frying

8 flour tortillas

1 recipe Vinegar Slaw (recipe follows) for serving

1. Rinse the fish fillets, pat dry, and cut into thin strips. Combine the panko and Cajun seasoning in a shallow dish. Combine the eggs, half-and-half, and a dash of the hot sauce in a separate dish. Dredge the fish strips in the egg mixture and then in the panko mixture, pressing well to adhere. Place the coated fish on a plate and let stand for 5 to 10 minutes to dry.

2. Place the yogurt, avocado, lime juice, cilantro, and a dash of the hot sauce in a blender or food processor and puree until smooth, stopping to scrape down the sides as needed. Set the sauce aside.

3. Pour the oil to a depth of 1 inch in a large, deep skillet and heat to 350°F. Fry the fish, in batches, for 1 to 2 minutes on each side, or until the fish flakes and is golden brown. Drain on paper towels.

4. Divide the fish between the tortillas and top with the slaw and avocado cream sauce. Serve.

Vinegar Slaw

I belong to the vinegar-based coleslaw camp, and this glorified dump-and-stir version pairs perfectly with Tom's crispy fish bites. Make this slaw in advance to allow the cabbage to soften and the flavors to meld.

1 (1-lb.) package shredded coleslaw mix

1 small red onion, halved and thinly sliced

1 jalapeño chile, seeded and finely chopped

3 Tbsp. olive oil

2 Tbsp. apple cider vinegar

Salt and freshly ground pepper

Combine the coleslaw mix, red onion, and jalapeño in a large bowl. Stir in the oil, vinegar, and salt and pepper to taste. Cover and refrigerate until ready to serve.

Corn Fritters with Hot 'n' Sweet Dipping Sauce

Fry up these babies and set them out with the dipping sauce while you're preparing the fish tacos, but maybe set aside a couple for yourself, because when you turn around, they'll be gone. Using fresh corn is always preferable, but if fresh corn isn't available, use frozen cream corn.

For the fritters:

8 ears corn, shucked, or 2 cups frozen
    cream corn, thawed
½ cup shredded sharp Cheddar
    cheese
¼ cup finely chopped green onions
¼ cup finely chopped onion
¼ cup milk
2 large eggs, lightly beaten
3 slices bacon, cooked and crumbled
½ tsp. minced garlic
1 cup all-purpose flour

½ cup plain cornmeal
1 Tbsp. baking powder
2 tsp. salt
2 tsp. freshly ground pepper
Canola oil for frying

For the dipping sauce:

1 cup mayonnaise
2 Tbsp. honey
1 Tbsp. hot sauce (or to taste)

1. Wrap the corn tightly in parchment or wax paper and microwave on high power for 4 minutes. When cool enough to handle, cut the corn off the cob into a bowl.

2. Stir in the cheese, green onions, onion, milk, eggs, bacon, and garlic. Combine the flour, cornmeal, baking powder, salt, and pepper in a separate bowl. Add to the corn mixture, and stir just until dry ingredients are moistened.

3. Pour the oil to a depth of 2 inches in a deep skillet and heat to 350°F.

4. Using a small ice cream or cookie scoop, drop the batter into the hot oil, and cook, in batches, for 3 to 5 minutes, turning once. Drain on paper towels and sprinkle with salt.

5. To make the dipping sauce, combine all the ingredients in a small bowl. Serve with the fritters.

Old School Mac 'n' Cheese

This is the one dish of mine that everybody in the family asks for. It's what I send to a new mom, a grieving friend, or a neighbor too busy to cook. Buy good, extra-sharp Cheddar cheese—what my ninety-something-year-old friend, Nanny, calls "rat cheese"—and shred it yourself. Make a double batch and freeze one in a disposable aluminum pan. Or, while you're grating all that cheese, go ahead and whomp up a bowl of Ritualistic Pimento Cheese (page 11)—another great make 'n' take.

1 lb. elbow macaroni

¼ cup (½ stick) salted butter, divided

3 Tbsp. all-purpose flour

1 to 1 ½ cups milk

½ tsp. salt

½ tsp. dry mustard

Freshly ground pepper

4 cups shredded extra-sharp Cheddar cheese, divided

½ cup panko bread crumbs

1. Preheat the oven to 350°F. Grease eight 5- to 6-ounce ramekins or a 2- to 3-quart baking dish. Bring a large pot of salted water to a boil, add the macaroni, and cook according to the package directions; drain.

2. Meanwhile, melt 3 tablespoons of the butter in a heavy saucepan over medium heat. Whisk in the flour and cook for 2 minutes, or until bubbly. Add 1 cup milk, and cook, stirring constantly, until the mixture is thickened. Add additional milk if you prefer a thinner cheese sauce.

3. Stir in the salt, the mustard, and the pepper to taste. Add 3 cups of the cheese and continue to cook over medium heat for 2 to 3 minutes, or until the cheese is melted.

4. Combine the cheese sauce and pasta. Pour the mixture into the prepared ramekins or dish. Sprinkle the panko and the remaining cheese over the macaroni. Top with the remaining 1 tablespoon butter.

5. Bake for 30 minutes, or until the topping is browned and the casserole is bubbly. Serve.

Frozen Key Lime Pie Pops

After I sampled a chocolate-covered frozen key lime bar on a book tour in Florida several years ago, I became obsessed with trying to find out where I COULD GET MORE. MORE. MORE. And then, fortunately, I forgot about these dark chocolate demons until it was time to dream up new beach house desserts. It took three tries to come up with this, the winning version. Should I admit that the first two tries involved using lime juice and uncooked egg yolks, plus sweetened condensed milk? And that it didn't occur to me that this could be a health hazard until AFTER my darling grandchildren had gobbled down my failures? The good news is, nobody got sick, probably because the acid in the lime juice "cooked" the yolks. I buy a bottled Key lime juice available at most grocery stores, but if you can't find Nellie & Joe's Key West Lime Juice, you can squeeze whatever limes you can find. Key limes, of course, are smallish, light green limes that are considerably more tart than regular Persian limes. For a fun twist, try drizzling the pops with that "magic" chocolate coating you can find with the ice cream toppings at the grocery store. This recipe uses a standard 10-pop mold, but feel free to make two batches in a 6-pop mold, or go old school and use paper cups and wooden craft sticks.

1 (14-oz.) can sweetened condensed milk

1 cup half-and-half

¾ cup bottled Key lime juice (we tested with Nellie & Joe's)

1 tsp. grated lime zest

1 drop green food coloring

1 drop yellow food coloring

Wooden craft sticks

1 cup graham cracker crumbs

1. Whisk the sweetened condensed milk, half-and-half, Key lime juice, lime zest, and food coloring together in a large liquid measuring cup.

2. Pour the mixture into ten 3-ounce ice pop molds, and insert the sticks. Freeze for 5 to 6 hours, or until frozen.

3. Spread the graham cracker crumbs in a shallow dish. Dip the molds in very warm water for 10 seconds. Unmold the ice pops, coat in graham cracker crumbs, and serve.

Full Moon Party

No matter how many times I view one, a full moon over the ocean still fills me with awe and wonder. On those lucky nights when we happen to be at Ebbtide and one occurs, I typically herd everybody down the long boardwalk over the dunes so they can see the moon reflected in the water. A couple of years ago, when I was at Bald Head Island, North Carolina, researching my novel The Weekenders, *my friend and I lucked into a full moon party. It later inspired a scene in the book, whose setting was in turn loosely inspired by Bald Head. For my own full moon celebration, I thought it was fitting to choose dishes that remind us of how blessed we are to live in such close proximity to the bountiful sea. You can prepare the tomatoes, mango salsa, green beans, beer bread, and even the ice cream sandwiches well ahead of time. After dinner is served, everybody can grab one of the ice cream sandwiches and an adult beverage before heading down to the beach for some moon dancing.*

SERVES 4

menu

Bloody Mary–Marinated Tomatoes

Crab Cakes with Mango Salsa

Lemon-Pecan Green Beans

Cheesy Beer Bread

Sweetie Pie Ice Cream Sandwiches

Bloody Mary–Marinated Tomatoes

I can't remember when I started making this recipe, but I do know I love it because no matter what time of year it is—even in the dead of winter—you can usually find decent cherry or grape tomatoes. I added the boiled shrimp, pickled okra, and bacon after being inspired by the colossal Bloody Marys served at AJ's Dockside Restaurant, a favorite sunset-watching and sipping spot on Tybee Island. If you'd like, keep the Bloody Mary image intact and wet the rim of a shallow serving dish, then dip it in Old Bay seasoning. Serve this with crusty bread to mop up the juices. If there are any leftovers, they're mighty tasty over scrambled eggs for breakfast.

1 pt. cherry or grape tomatoes, halved

8 oz. medium shrimp, cooked and peeled

8 pickled okra, halved lengthwise, plus 2 Tbsp. pickled okra juice, divided

2 stalks celery, coarsely chopped

Grated zest and juice of 1 large lemon

1 Tbsp. vodka

1 Tbsp. extra-virgin olive oil

2 tsp. Worcestershire sauce

1 clove garlic, minced

Pinch of celery salt

Hot sauce

Sea salt and freshly ground pepper

4 oz. blue cheese, crumbled

3 slices thick-cut bacon, cooked and coarsely crumbled

Crusty French or Italian bread, sliced, for serving

1. Combine the tomatoes, shrimp, okra, and celery in a large bowl.

2. In a separate bowl, whisk the okra juice, lemon zest and juice, vodka, oil, Worcestershire sauce, garlic, and celery salt together, and then season with hot sauce, salt, and pepper to taste. Pour over the tomato mixture, stirring to coat. Cover and refrigerate for at least 1 hour.

3. Sprinkle the tomato mixture with the cheese and bacon, and serve with the bread.

Crab Cakes with Mango Salsa

The cookbooks of Martha Giddens Nesbit, longtime food editor and columnist in Savannah, are ones south Georgia cooks turn to more often than that "other" Martha. Her crab cake recipe was the inspiration for Tom's recipe, and she's also my go-to resource for all things concerning Low Country cuisine. If mangoes aren't available for the salsa, we also serve these crab cakes with a quick topper made from mayonnaise and bottled chili sauce.

3 Tbsp. olive oil, divided

1 small red bell pepper, finely chopped

1 shallot, finely diced

1 green onion, finely chopped

1 clove garlic, minced

3 Tbsp. half-and-half

1 Tbsp. Dijon mustard

Cayenne pepper

1 large egg, lightly beaten

1 cup panko bread crumbs, divided

8 oz. lump crabmeat, picked over

8 oz. claw crabmeat, picked over

½ cup freshly grated Parmigiano-Reggiano cheese

2 Tbsp. (¼ stick) salted butter

1 recipe Mango Salsa (recipe follows) for serving

1. Heat 1 tablespoon of the oil in a medium skillet over medium-high heat. Add the bell pepper, shallot, green onion, and garlic, and sauté for 3 minutes, or until tender.

2. Transfer the mixture to a bowl and stir in the half-and-half, mustard, and cayenne pepper to taste. Add the egg and ½ cup of the panko and mix well. Gently fold in the crabmeat.

3. Line a rimmed baking sheet with parchment paper, and shape the mixture into eight ½-inch-thick crab cakes.

4. Combine the remaining ½ cup panko and the cheese. Coat the crab cakes on both sides in the panko mixture and place on the prepared baking sheet. Cover and refrigerate for at least 2 hours.

5. Heat the remaining 2 tablespoons oil and the butter in a heavy skillet over medium-high heat. Cook the crab cakes, in batches, 4 to 5 minutes on each side, or until golden brown. Serve with the salsa.

Mango Salsa

I developed this recipe to be served with Tom's crab cakes, but it's also delicious served with grilled chicken, fish, or pork. If you're not a cilantro fan, substitute chopped parsley and add or omit the jalapeño and serrano chiles according to your preferences. Make it early in the day and chill for several hours to give the flavors time to blend.

2 ripe mangoes, peeled and diced

½ cored pineapple, diced

1 small red onion, diced

1 small red bell pepper, diced

1 jalapeño chile, seeded and finely diced

1 small serrano chile, seeded and finely diced

3 Tbsp. chopped fresh cilantro

¼ cup rice vinegar

Grated zest and juice of 1 lime

1 Tbsp. olive oil

1 tsp. salt

¼ tsp. freshly ground black pepper

1. Combine the mangoes, pineapple, onion, bell pepper, jalapeño, serrano, and cilantro in a large bowl.

2. Whisk the vinegar, lime zest and juice, oil, salt, and pepper together in a small bowl, and pour over the salsa, mixing well. Cover and refrigerate until ready to serve.

Lemon-Pecan Green Beans

In theory, there is something comforting and old school about sitting in the kitchen, snapping green beans, sipping iced tea (or chilled wine), and passing the time with my family. But I will confess that sometimes, when I'm in a hurry or preparing a multicourse dinner, I buy the bagged, trimmed, and washed green beans in the produce section and just drink the wine and pretend that I'm overworked.

¾ cup pecan halves and pieces

2 lb. green beans, trimmed

5 Tbsp. (about ⅓ stick)
   unsalted butter

2 shallots, finely chopped

2 tsp. grated lemon zest plus 1 Tbsp.
   juice (1 lemon)

1 tsp. sea salt

1. Preheat the oven to 350°F. Arrange the pecans in a single layer on a rimmed baking sheet, and bake for 6 to 8 minutes, or until toasted. Set aside.

2. Bring the green beans in water to cover to a boil in a large stockpot. Cook for 5 minutes, or until tender. Drain and then plunge in an ice water bath to stop cooking. Drain well, and dry on paper towels.

3. Melt the butter in a large skillet over medium-high heat. Add the shallots and cook for 2 to 3 minutes, stirring constantly. Reduce the heat to medium, add the beans, and cook for 5 minutes, or until thoroughly heated. Stir in the toasted pecans, lemon zest and juice, and salt and cook for 1 minute longer. Serve.

Cheesy Beer Bread

In a perfect world, I would have inherited my Irish grandmother's bread-baking skills. Mary Ellen Hogan, or Nanny, as we called her, would arrive in St. Petersburg from her home in Chicago every May, just in time to spend Mother's Day with her only son's family and to watch one of us make our First Holy Communion. As a small child, I would sit on her bed and watch with fascination as she unpacked her valise, as she called it, which contained her good Sunday black, blue, or brown dresses; rosary; travel-size bottle of holy water; starched apron; and cake of yeast. She always brought her own yeast because she was deeply suspicious of Florida yeast. Almost every morning of her two-week visit, she would make two loaves of her perfect bread, which she would slice, butter, and then drizzle with honey. I was blessed to get Nanny's thick, curly hair and cursed with her thick, sturdy ankles. But the bread-baking gene is lacking in my DNA. Instead, when the occasion arises, I make quick breads like this one. And my family still seems to love me, despite my yeast-bread-baking deficiency.

3 cups self-rising flour

½ cup sugar

½ cup shredded sharp Cheddar
   cheese

1 (12-oz.) can light beer

2 Tbsp. (¼ stick) salted butter,
   melted

1. Preheat the oven to 350°F. Grease a 9-by-5-inch loaf pan. Combine the flour, sugar, and cheese in a medium bowl. Add the beer and stir until combined. Pour the batter into the prepared pan.

2. Bake for 50 minutes. Brush with the melted butter and bake for 10 minutes longer, or until a wooden pick inserted in the center comes out clean and the top is browned. Let cool in the pan for 10 minutes, turn out onto a wire rack, and serve warm, or let cool until ready to serve.

Sweetie Pie Ice Cream Sandwiches

My friend Susan Kelleher, who owns a gelato emporium and candy shop called Seaside Sweets on Tybee Island, came up with the idea of making cookie-gelato sandwiches she called Sweetie Pies. She even named her gelato trailer Sweetie Pie. You need a sturdy but chewy cookie to withstand crumbling into the ice cream or gelato, and I had just the cookie recipe to do the trick. Think of this oatmeal-based cookie as the little black dress of desserts. You can make it with raisins—although my daughter Katie would object to that—or with chocolate chips, like I call for here. The first time I tested this recipe with Molly and Griffin, I only had butterscotch chips, and they were great. You could also use your favorite chopped-up candy bar. As for the ice cream filling—we show coffee here, but the sky's the limit. Molly suggests that you do roll the ice-creamed edges of the finished sweetie pie in a shallow dish of sprinkles. Because sprinkles make everything better. Except maybe vodka.

1 cup (2 sticks) unsalted butter,
   softened
1 cup firmly packed light brown
   sugar
½ cup granulated sugar
1 large egg plus 1 large egg yolk
1 Tbsp. vanilla extract
2 cups all-purpose flour

1 cup old-fashioned oats
1 tsp. baking powder
1 tsp. baking soda
1 tsp. kosher salt
3 cups semi-sweet chocolate chips
1 qt. ice cream, softened
Sprinkles

1. Preheat the oven to 325°F. Beat the butter and both sugars with an electric mixer until creamy. Add the egg and egg yolk and beat until combined. Beat in the vanilla.

2. Combine the flour, oats, baking powder, baking soda, and salt in a bowl. Gradually add to the butter mixture, beating until combined. Stir in the chocolate chips. (The dough will be thick.)

3. Using a 2-tablespoon cookie scoop, scoop the dough into 24 balls and drop onto parchment paper–lined baking sheets, leaving about 1 ½ inches between the cookies.

4. Bake for 22 to 25 minutes, or until the cookies are lightly browned. Transfer to wire racks to cool.

5. Place a scoop of ice cream between two cookies and press to allow the ice cream to reach the cookie edges. Roll in your favorite sprinkles, wrap with plastic, and freeze until firm. Serve.

Game Day Dinner

Fall is one of our favorite times to be at the beach—fewer crowds, cooler temps, and yes, football. On Saturday afternoons, this University of Georgia grad is all Bulldog, and my ramblin' wreck of a husband and Georgia Tech alum is rooting for the rival Yellow Jackets. But instead of packing up and driving to Athens or Atlanta, we just tailgate on the downstairs porch at Ebbtide, where the grill is handy. A few years ago, when I was working on Spring Fever, I spent some time in Salisbury, North Carolina, the home of Cheerwine, which is a distinctive-tasting cherry cola made by a small family-owned company. Try these Cheerwine-glazed ribs and you'll be won over. As the ribs (or pork butt) are cooking, we turn the televisions to all the main games being followed by our guests, and everybody's happy. And there are no long treks to the stadium bathroom or parking snarls.

SERVES 8 TO 10

menu

Nene's Beergaritas

Black Bean and Corn Salsa

Smoked Pork Butt with Beach House Barbecue Sauce

Dry Rub

Cherrylicious Glazed Ribs

Boy Howdy Baked Beans

Broccoli Salad

Dot's Congo Bars

Nene's Beergaritas

No trip to the beach would be complete for my family without a thermos of the icy deliciousness of Nene's Beergaritas, created and perfected by my sister-in-law Jeanne Trocheck, who is called Nene by her adoring nieces and nephews. Serve in a festive pitcher, and prepare to make another trip to the store for more limeade.

2 (12-oz.) cans frozen limeade
    concentrate

2 (12-oz.) bottles light Mexican beer

2 (8-oz.) cans lemon-lime soda

1 ½ cups tequila

Margarita salt

Lime wedges, for serving

Stir the limeade concentrate, beer, soda, and tequila together in a pitcher. Pour into ice-filled glasses rimmed with the margarita salt, and serve with the lime wedges.

Black Bean and Corn Salsa

You know a recipe is well loved when the handwritten card for it is splattered with tomato seeds and vinaigrette drippings. This has long been a favorite at the neighborhood pool among certain parties who sit under a particular umbrella sipping margaritas, eating salsa and tortilla chips, and talking trash. No names, please!

1 (15.5-oz.) can black beans, drained and rinsed

1 ½ cups cooked fresh corn kernels (about 4 ears)

2 tomatoes, diced

1 red bell pepper, diced

1 green bell pepper, diced

½ cup finely diced red onion

2 serrano chiles, seeded and minced

⅓ cup fresh lime juice (3 limes)

⅓ cup olive oil

¼ cup finely chopped fresh cilantro

1 tsp. sea salt

½ tsp. ground cumin

½ tsp. cayenne pepper

Tortilla chips, for serving

1. Combine the beans, corn, tomatoes, bell peppers, onion, and serranos in a medium bowl.

2. Whisk together the lime juice, oil, cilantro, salt, cumin, and cayenne pepper in a small bowl. Pour over the black bean mixture and stir well. Cover and refrigerate until ready to serve. Serve with the tortilla chips.

Smoked Pork Butt with Beach House Barbecue Sauce

Throughout the year, on all but the rainiest weekends, the scent of smoking meat is a constant in our Atlanta neighborhood, where firing up smokers has become somewhat of a spectator sport. Tom is definitely a member of Team Big Green Egg, especially because most of the time, he can put something on the smoker early in the morning, check on it occasionally, and still manage to get in some other manly sport. However, he assures me that if you are not a competitive smoker, you can still produce a quality smoked pork butt simply by baking it in a covered Dutch oven at 300°F. For a four- to six-pound roast, figure on three to four hours, or until the meat is fork-tender. We like to serve our pulled pork with a riff on the bottled sauce from Johnny Harris, a restaurant in Savannah that closed last year after ninety-two years in business. Johnny Harris was our date-night destination when we were newlyweds living on a tight budget, and where for years a group of Savannah Morning News *alums met for lunch. The sauce recipe makes a bunch—about 10 to 12 cups—so pour it into sterilized bottles or jars and keep or share.*

For the pork butt:
1 (4- to 6-lb.) pork butt or shoulder
1 cup Dry Rub (recipe follows)
12 sandwich buns

For the barbecue sauce:
6 cups ketchup
6 cups apple cider vinegar
1 (10-oz.) bottle Worcestershire
    sauce

¾ cup firmly packed brown sugar
⅔ cup dry mustard
½ cup (1 stick) unsalted butter
6 Tbsp. freshly ground pepper
¼ cup hot sauce (we tested with
    Texas Pete)
3 Tbsp. sea salt

1. Prepare a charcoal fire in a smoker according to the manufacturer's instructions. Place the water pan in the smoker; add water to the depth of the fill line. Regulate the temperature with a thermometer to between 230°F and 260°F for 10 minutes.

2. Rub the pork butt with the Dry Rub. Place on the upper food grate and close the smoker. Smoke for 4 to 6 hours, or until a meat thermometer inserted in the thickest portion registers 200°F.

3. Remove the pork from the smoker, cover with foil, and let rest for 30 minutes.

4. To make the barbecue sauce, combine all the ingredients in a large stockpot over medium-high heat. Bring to a boil, reduce the heat to medium, and simmer for 30 minutes, or until thickened.

5. Pull the meat into pieces using two forks. Serve on the buns topped with desired amount of barbecue sauce. Refrigerate extra sauce for up to three months.

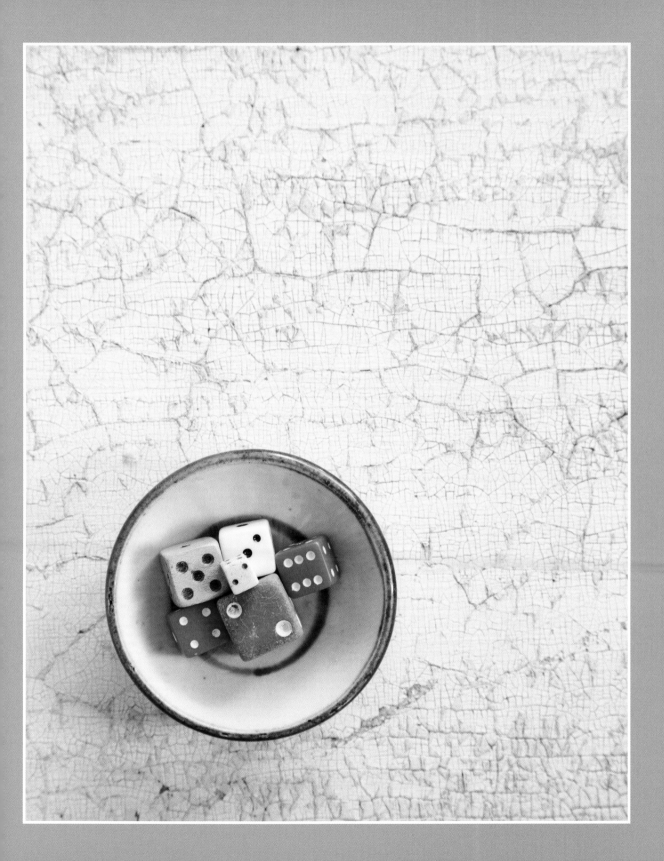

Dry Rub

This flavor-packed rub makes a hefty amount—about 1 ½ cups. Store leftovers in an airtight container.

½ cup chili powder

½ cup firmly packed light brown
    sugar

¼ cup paprika

1 Tbsp. garlic powder

1 Tbsp. onion powder

1 Tbsp. ground cumin

2 tsp. freshly ground black pepper

2 tsp. cayenne pepper

2 tsp. dry mustard

1 tsp. salt

Combine all the ingredients in a medium bowl.

Cherrylicious Glazed Ribs

My novel Spring Fever *is set at a small, family-owned company that manufactures a fictitious soft drink called Quixie. To research the book, I traveled to Salisbury, North Carolina, the home of Cheerwine, a delicious cherry-flavored soft drink. Use a disposable aluminum foil baking pan for easy cleanup. P.S. If some soda should find its way into a tall glass filled with crushed ice and rum, that would not be an altogether bad thing.*

For the ribs:

1 Tbsp. dark brown sugar

2 tsp. kosher salt

1 tsp. coarsely ground pepper

1 tsp. chili powder

1 tsp. paprika

4 lb. pork baby back ribs

4 cups cherry-flavored soda (we tested with Cheerwine)

For the glaze:

1 (12-oz.) can cherry-flavored soda (we tested with Cheerwine)

½ cup red pepper jelly

¼ cup Worcestershire sauce

¼ apple cider vinegar

¼ cup tomato paste

¼ cup Dijon mustard

3 Tbsp. soy sauce

2 cloves garlic, minced

1. Preheat the oven to 400°F. Combine the dry ingredients. Rub all over the ribs and place them meaty-side up on a rack in a large roasting pan. Pour the soda into the pan and cover tightly with aluminum foil.

2. Bake the ribs for about 1 hour and 45 minutes, or until very tender.

3. Meanwhile, combine the glaze ingredients in a medium saucepan and cook over medium heat for 20 to 25 minutes, stirring occasionally, until liquid is reduced and mixture is syrupy.

4. Uncover the ribs and remove them from the pan. Pour off the fat and liquid from the pan and discard.

5. Turn the oven to broil. Brush the ribs with the glaze and return to the rack in the pan, meaty-side up. Broil about 8 inches from the heat for 5 minutes, or until the glaze begins to brown. Serve with additional glaze on the side.

Boy Howdy Baked Beans

Among our circle of friends, bourbon is practically its own food group. We like it for baking, we like it for sauces, and we especially like it for sipping. Our friend Dave even got a special ice machine that makes crushed ice for his nightly libation. Now, I might be run out of town on a rail for saying this, but I suggest you keep the expensive, small-batch bourbon for sipping and buy a cheaper brand for casseroles like this.

2 (28-oz.) cans baked beans

½ cup firmly packed dark brown
    sugar

¼ cup tomato-based barbecue sauce

¼ cup maple sugar

¼ cup bourbon

1 small onion, chopped

2 Tbsp. grainy mustard

8 slices maple bacon, cooked and
    crumbled

1. Preheat the oven to 350°F. Combine all the ingredients except the bacon in a greased 2-quart baking dish. Bake for 45 minutes, or until the edges begin to bubble.
2. Sprinkle with the crumbled bacon and cook for 15 minutes longer. Serve.

Broccoli Salad

This recipe has been kicking around my files as Holiday Broccoli Salad forever. Maybe because the ingredients include dried cranberries? But why should the holidays get all the fun? This is even easier to make these days, what with bags of precut broccoli florets available in the produce section and precooked bacon slices sold in the meat department. Some recipes I've seen use raw broccoli, but I like my broccoli barely blanched.

2 (12-oz.) bags broccoli florets

¾ cup dried sweetened cranberries

½ cup pecans, toasted

½ cup shelled, roasted and salted
    sunflower seeds

½ cup diced red onion

2 slices bacon, cooked and finely
    crumbled

1 cup mayonnaise

3 Tbsp. sugar

Grated zest and juice of 1 lemon

1 Tbsp. rice vinegar

1 ½ tsp. poppy seeds

¼ tsp. sea salt

Freshly ground pepper

1. Bring a large pot of salted water to a boil. Add the broccoli and cook for 30 seconds. Drain and plunge into an ice water bath to stop cooking. Drain again, and pat dry with paper towels.

2. Combine the broccoli, cranberries, pecans, sunflower seeds, onion, and bacon in a large serving bowl.

3. Whisk together the mayonnaise, the sugar, the lemon zest and juice, the vinegar, the poppy seeds, the salt, and pepper to taste in a small bowl until combined. Pour the dressing over the broccoli mixture and toss well to coat. Cover and refrigerate until ready to serve.

Dot's Congo Bars

My mother-in-law, Dot, was a prolific baker, especially of cookies. Every fall she would start clipping coupons and plan her holiday baking, and just before Christmas she would produce miraculous cookie trays with at least a dozen different varieties of fancy cookies, which she gifted to everybody from the mailman to neighbors to family and church friends, all of whom eagerly anticipated this annual Christmas gift. But my own family's favorite of Dot's cookies are these sturdy oatmeal and chocolate bars. They always remind her grandchildren of their Grammy, who punctuated almost every sentence with a heartfelt "Thank God, honey."

1 (12-oz.) package semisweet
    chocolate chips

1 cup milk

1 cup plus 1 Tbsp. (about 2 ⅛ sticks)
    salted butter, softened, divided

2 ⅔ cups firmly packed brown sugar

2 large eggs

3 cups old-fashioned oats

2 ½ cups all-purpose flour

1 tsp. baking soda

1 tsp. salt

1. Preheat the oven to 350°F. Combine the chocolate chips, milk, and 1 tablespoon of the butter in a microwave-safe bowl. Microwave on high power for 1 minute and stir. Microwave at 30-second intervals until the chocolate melts and the mixture is smooth. Set aside.

2. Beat the remaining 1 cup butter and the brown sugar with an electric mixer until creamy. Add the eggs, one at a time, beating just until the yellow disappears.

3. Stir together the oats, flour, baking soda, and salt. Add to the butter mixture, beating until combined. Press two-thirds of the dough into a greased jelly roll pan.

4. Pour the melted chocolate mixture over the dough. Butter your hands and then flatten tablespoon-size scoops of the remaining dough into thin disks. Arrange over the chocolate mixture in a polka-dot pattern.

5. Bake for 20 to 30 minutes, or until set. Let cool completely in the pan on a wire rack. Cut into bars and serve.

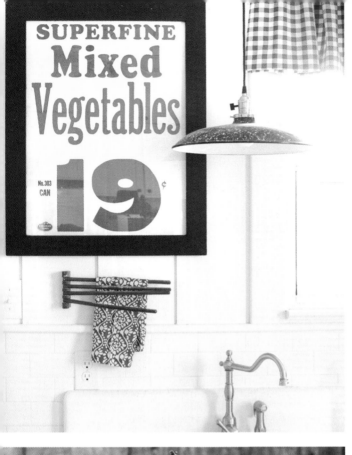

Souper Supper

On the first really cold night at the beach, Tom and I will sometimes decide to make dueling soups. We "light" the electric stove in our fireplace, put on some mellow oldies tunes, and before long, good smells start wafting throughout the house. He likes his food spicy and I don't, so to alleviate the bickering and backbiting in the kitchen, we decided we'd each make our own soup and let friends decide which is best. Funny, everybody is always eager to sample, but they fall silent when it's time to vote. The best thing about a meal like this is that you can make the soups ahead of time and keep them warm in slow cookers. The soup recipes make approximately eight servings each, but they are also easily doubled, so sometimes we make enough to send home a batch with our guests. We rotate the soups, but here are a few that have been declared winners by popular vote.

SERVES 8

menu

Romaine Salad with Pink Grapefruit,
Avocado, and Goat Cheese

Black Bean Soup

Jalapeño Cornbread

Corn and Crab Chowder

Roasted Veggie Soup

Mini Grilled Cheese Sandwiches

Boomerang Boy's Apple Crisp

Romaine Salad with Pink Grapefruit, Avocado, and Goat Cheese

This salad always reminds me of barefoot days growing up in Florida. Almost every yard in our neighborhood had citrus trees, but our friends the Bests also had a towering avocado tree that produced huge, glossy, lime-green avocados, which we would slice open, squeeze with lime juice from another neighbor's tree, and eat, out of hand, sprinkled with salt. I'll confess that these days, I usually buy the refrigerated jars of already-sectioned grapefruit in the produce section, which gives me plenty of juice for the citrus dressing.

For the salad:

2 heads romaine lettuce, coarsely chopped

2 cups pink grapefruit sections

2 avocados, pitted and sliced

1 small red onion, thinly sliced

1 (4-oz.) log goat cheese, crumbled

For the dressing:

6 Tbsp. canola oil

¼ cup pink grapefruit juice

2 Tbsp. honey

1 tsp. Dijon mustard

Kosher salt and freshly ground pepper to taste

1. Combine the lettuce, grapefruit, avocados, and onion in a large shallow salad bowl. Sprinkle with the goat cheese.

2. For the dressing, place the remaining ingredients, including salt and pepper to taste, in a jar with a tight-fitting lid. Seal and shake well to combine.

3. Drizzle the salad with the dressing and serve.

Black Bean Soup

As a child, I had a pathological aversion to all kinds of peas and beans, so much so that I would sit at the dinner table for hours after the rest of the family had eaten, staring stubbornly down at the hated pile of canned Le Sueur peas remaining on my dinner plate. Eventually, though, I did see the light. Now I love making this Cuban-inspired dish on cold winter nights, especially when I have a nice meaty ham bone to throw in the soup pot. Sometimes I buy the bones that have been cut off spiral-sliced hams at the supermarket or those specialty honey-baked ham shops. You can simmer this in a soup kettle on top of the stove over low heat, or start it early in the morning in a slow cooker. Some recipes call for putting half the soup in a blender to achieve the proper balance of blended to whole beans, but this is where I love to use my immersion blender. They're inexpensive and indispensable, so I keep one at the beach and one at home. Serve this soup with an assortment of toppings like sour cream, shredded Cheddar cheese, and fresh cilantro.

3 Tbsp. olive oil

1 onion, finely chopped

1 red bell pepper, finely chopped

2 cloves garlic, minced

1 meaty ham bone or smoked ham hock

3 (15.5-oz.) cans black beans, drained and rinsed

3 ½ cups beef broth

1 (10-oz.) can diced tomatoes with green chiles

1 tsp. ground cumin

Salt and freshly ground black pepper

1. Heat the oil in a Dutch oven over medium-high heat. Add the onion and bell pepper and sauté for 5 minutes or until tender. Add the garlic and sauté for 2 minutes longer.

2. Add the ham bone, beans, broth, tomatoes, and cumin. Bring to a boil; reduce the heat, and simmer for 30 minutes, stirring occasionally.

3. Remove from the heat and discard the ham bone. Using an immersion blender, puree the soup to reach the desired thickness, leaving some beans whole (or puree a portion of the soup in a blender and return it to the pot). Season with the salt and pepper to taste, and serve.

Jalapeño Cornbread

Convenience food alert! I'll admit it: This recipe is full of shortcuts that time-challenged cooks will love and foodie purists will hate—until they take a taste. And then I will be vindicated.

1 (8.5-oz.) package cornbread mix

1 (8.5-oz.) can cream-style corn

½ cup shredded Mexican-blend cheese

¼ cup milk

1 large egg

1 jalapeño chile, seeded and minced

1. Place a greased 12-inch cast-iron skillet in the oven and preheat the oven to 400°F.

2. Whisk all ingredients together in a bowl. Pour into the hot skillet. Bake for 15 to 20 minutes, or until the cornbread is golden brown and a toothpick inserted in the center comes out clean. Serve.

Corn and Crab Chowder

Very few of the soups I make hew closely to a written recipe—especially when we're at the beach, where I might not have all the ingredients my recipe calls for on hand. This corn and crab chowder is a good example. Sometimes I leave the potatoes out if I don't have any. Sometimes I substitute cream or whole milk for the half-and-half, and sometimes I use frozen corn—I like the kind that comes frozen in a tube—but in the summer, I prefer to use fresh corn. I do always use crab; usually claw meat, since in a soup you really can't distinguish lump from claw. And I love the deep flavor the shot of sherry adds at the end. If you like a thicker chowder, whisk 1 tablespoon all-purpose flour with 2 tablespoons half-and-half and stir it into the soup at the end, before adding the sherry. Simmer for 5 minutes to thicken.

1 Tbsp. olive oil, plus extra as needed

2 slices bacon

2 large shallots, minced

1 small red bell pepper, chopped

6 small red potatoes, unpeeled, cut into ½-inch cubes

3 cups fresh corn kernels (about 8 ears)

1 ¾ cups low-sodium chicken broth

1 cup half-and-half

1 lb. crabmeat, picked over

¼ cup dry sherry

1 tsp. sea salt

Freshly ground black pepper

Chopped chives for garnish

1. Heat 1 tablespoon oil in a Dutch oven over medium heat, add the bacon, and cook for 8 minutes, or until crisp. Transfer the bacon to paper towels to drain, and reserve the drippings in the pot. Chop the bacon.

2. Sauté the shallots and bell pepper in the bacon drippings for 3 minutes, or until tender, adding more oil if there aren't enough drippings. Add the potatoes and sauté for 5 minutes.

3. Stir in the corn, broth, and half-and-half and simmer over medium-low heat for about 30 minutes, stirring occasionally, until the potatoes are tender. Stir in the crabmeat and cook 5 minutes longer. Remove from the heat, stir in the sherry and salt and season with the pepper to taste. Garnish with the bacon and chives. Serve.

Roasted Veggie Soup

One of my favorite lunch spots in Atlanta, especially when I'm craving healthy food, is Souper Jenny in downtown Decatur. The restaurant features at least half a dozen made-from-scratch daily soups, as well as imaginative salads and sandwiches. Here's my version of Souper Jenny's Absolutely Everything Roasted Veggie Soup recipe, which was published in the Atlanta Journal-Constitution some years ago. The ready-to-serve bagged vegetables I find in the produce section of local supermarkets these days make this so much quicker to put together. I buy the already peeled and cubed packets of butternut squash, the presnapped green beans, and the cartons of sliced mushrooms. This is also a great "clean-out-the-fridge" soup when you have odds and ends of leftover veggies.

1 (16-oz.) package sliced mushrooms

2 cups (2-inch slices) green beans

1 cup baby carrots

1 cup diced parsnips

1 cup cubed butternut squash

1 cup coarsely chopped red onion

1 bunch asparagus, tips only

3 Tbsp. olive oil

12 cups low-sodium chicken or vegetable broth

1 (28-oz.) can crushed tomatoes

1 bay leaf

1 zucchini, diced

1 yellow squash, diced

1 (5-oz.) package baby kale mix

Kosher salt and freshly ground pepper

1. Preheat the oven to 425°F. Place the mushrooms, green beans, carrots, parsnips, squash, onion, and asparagus on a rimmed baking sheet, drizzle the oil over the vegetables, and toss to coat. Roast for 15 to 20 minutes, or until the vegetables begin to brown around the edges.

2. While the vegetables roast, bring the broth, tomatoes, and bay leaf to a boil in a stockpot over medium-high heat. Stir in the roasted vegetables, zucchini, yellow squash, and kale. Return to a boil; reduce the heat to medium and simmer for 10 minutes, or until the zucchini and squash are tender. Season with the salt and pepper to taste, and serve.

Boomerang Boy's Apple Crisp

I nicknamed Andy "Boomerang Boy" because for several years he'd move away and then come back home. Repeatedly. The source for this recipe, his favorite dessert, is the school lunchroom at Lakewood High School in my hometown of St. Petersburg, Florida, where Tom and I met. The brown sugar–oat topping for this fresh apple concoction was so thick and crisp, you practically had to jackhammer it to get at the fruit. Over the years, I've actually quadrupled the topping recipe from my original rendition in order to reach maximum crisp nirvana. Make this with tart apples—I like Pink Ladies, which are grown in the north Georgia mountains, or Granny Smiths. You can use a buttered 3-quart baking dish instead of the miniature skillets if you prefer; just drizzle ½ cup water over the dish in step 2. And add 5 to 10 minutes to the cooking time.

6 cups peeled, sliced Granny Smith
    or Pink Lady apples

2 Tbsp. fresh lemon juice

1 cup firmly packed brown sugar

1 cup quick-cooking oats

¾ cup all-purpose flour

1 tsp. ground cinnamon

¼ tsp. grated nutmeg

¼ tsp. salt

½ cup (1 stick) salted butter, softened

Vanilla ice cream for serving

1. Preheat the oven to 350°F. Butter eight miniature 5- to 6-inch cast-iron skillets.

2. Toss the apples and lemon juice together in a large bowl. Divide the mixture evenly between the prepared cast-iron skillets. Drizzle 1 tablespoon water over each skillet.

3. Combine the brown sugar, oats, flour, cinnamon, nutmeg, and salt in a bowl. Cut in the butter with a pastry blender or two forks until the mixture is crumbly. Sprinkle the topping over the apples.

4. Bake for 30 to 35 minutes, or until the apples are tender and the topping is browned. Top with the vanilla ice cream and serve.

Thanksgiving at the Beach

It's often still warm enough in November at Tybee to take a long walk along the shore after stuffing ourselves, or if we're in Atlanta, to at least have appetizers outside—along with televised football games, of course. Wherever we are reminding ourselves of our many blessings, we do this holiday as a family potluck. Tom and his nephews each make dueling turkeys—we like ours brined and oven-roasted, because that method guarantees maximum gravy output. Zack and Alex usually deep-fry theirs in peanut oil. My sister-in-law Jeanne is the appetizer queen. Bacon-kissed green beans are another mandated menu item, as is my boozy bourbon sweet potato soufflé. The list of desserts our family devours at every holiday is truly embarrassing, but suffice it to say we always have Andy's pumpkin pie, augmented by pecan pie.

SERVES 8 TO 10

menu

Jeanne's Chicken Enchilada Dip

Tom Turkey

Boozy Sweet Potato Soufflé

Edna's Green Beans

Cranberry-Orange Chutney

Mashed Potatoes and Great Gravy

Pecan Pie

Andy's Personal Pumpkin Pie

Jeanne's Chicken Enchilada Dip

My sister-in-law Jeanne never arrives at any family function without a cooler full of appetizers, and this addictive cream cheese and chicken–based dip is always the superstar at any get-together. Covered and refrigerated, it stores well for up to a week. Be sure to choose sturdy tortilla chips to scoop up all the goodness.

3 large bone-in chicken breasts

1 lb. cream cheese, softened

1 ½ cups shredded sharp Cheddar
cheese

1 ½ Tbsp. chili powder

1 Tbsp. hot sauce, or to taste

1 tsp. minced garlic

1 tsp. ground cumin

1 tsp. dried oregano

1 tsp. paprika

1 (10-oz.) can diced tomatoes with
green chiles, undrained

½ cup chopped fresh cilantro, plus
extra for serving (optional)

4 green onions, chopped

Tortilla chips for serving

1. Place the chicken in a large stockpot, add water to cover, and bring to a boil. Reduce the heat and simmer for 20 to 30 minutes, or until the chicken is done. Remove the chicken from the water and let cool until easy to handle. Skin and debone the chicken, and shred the meat with two forks.

2. Beat the cream cheese with an electric mixer until creamy. Beat in the Cheddar, chili powder, hot sauce, garlic, cumin, oregano, and paprika. Stir in the chicken, tomatoes, cilantro, and green onions. Cover and refrigerate overnight.

3. Sprinkle the dip with additional cilantro, if desired, and serve with the tortilla chips.

Tom Turkey

See how I did that? Tom is my spousal unit, and this is his recipe. A male turkey . . . never mind. For years, Tom searched for the best method to achieve roast turkey nirvana. After he saw Martha Stewart demonstrating her brining technique on television, he was sold on brining. Over the years, he's tweaked and revised. This was his most recent creation. Next year could be different. Since our family is usually dining on TWO turkeys, each team cooks a 12- to 14-pound bird, allowing plenty of leftovers for everybody. You'll need some specialized equipment to achieve this: a very large stockpot, a plastic turkey brining bag, and a container big enough to chill the turkey overnight. We use our large cooler and a 5-pound bag of ice, but a large lidded plastic storage bin would also work. You'll also need a large piece of cheesecloth about the size of the turkey, with some overlap, and a large roasting pan with a rack.

1 (12- to 14-lb.) fresh or thawed
    frozen turkey

1 recipe Turkey Brine (recipe
    follows)

1 Tbsp. kosher salt

1 Tbsp. freshly ground pepper

6 Tbsp. (¾ stick) salted butter,
    softened, divided

2 cups dry white wine

4 cloves garlic, divided

2 onions, peeled and cut into large
    chunks

2 apples, quartered, plus apple
    wedges for serving (optional)

3 Tbsp. chopped fresh sage, plus
    whole sage leaves for serving
    (optional)

1 Tbsp. fresh thyme leaves

Fresh rosemary (optional)

1. Remove the giblets and neck from the turkey and set aside. Rinse the turkey and pat dry. Place the turkey inside the brining bag and then in a large container. Carefully pour the brine over the turkey in the bag, seal tightly, and refrigerate for 24 hours.

2. Set an oven rack in the lowest position, and preheat the oven to 375°F. Remove the turkey from the brine, pat dry, and place, breast side up, on a rack in a large roasting pan. Lift the wing tips up and over the back, and tuck under the turkey. Combine the kosher salt and pepper; sprinkle half of the mixture inside the turkey cavity.

3. Melt 2 tablespoons of the butter in a medium saucepan, and stir in the white wine. Immerse a 15-by-18-inch-size piece of cheesecloth in the wine mixture.

4. Mince 2 of the garlic cloves. Combine the remaining 4 tablespoons softened butter and the minced garlic. Starting at the neck cavity, loosen the skin from the turkey breast and drumsticks by inserting your fingers, gently pushing between the skin and meat. Rub the butter mixture under the loosened skin.

5. Place the onions, apples, and remaining garlic cloves inside the cavity. Tie the legs together with kitchen twine. Sprinkle the turkey with the remaining salt mixture and drape the wine-soaked cheesecloth over the skin, reserving the remainder of the wine mixture to brush on the turkey during roasting.

6. Roast for 1 hour and 30 minutes; add the giblets and neck to the roasting pan. Roast 30 minutes longer; remove the cheesecloth to promote browning. Roast 30 minutes longer, basting every 15 minutes, until a meat thermometer inserted in the meaty part of the thigh registers at least 170°F. Remove from the oven and let rest for 20 to 30 minutes before carving. Arrange the carved turkey on a platter, garnish with the apple wedges, sage, thyme, and rosemary, if desired, and serve.

TURKEY BRINE

1 cup kosher salt	1 Tbsp. onion powder
2 onions, coarsely chopped	2 sprigs fresh rosemary
1 (750-ml) bottle dry white wine	6 sprigs fresh thyme
¼ cup peppercorns	1 tsp. mustard seeds
2 Tbsp. coriander seeds	2 heads garlic, crushed

Place all the ingredients in a large stockpot, add 6 quarts water, and bring to a boil. Cook and stir until the salt dissolves. Let cool completely.

Boozy Sweet Potato Soufflé

This was my dad's favorite Thanksgiving recipe, well, aside from my mom's turkey gravy, which, come to think of it, used a healthy splash of white wine. Some folks might look at this as a dessert, but in the South, we just call it a side dish.

5 lb. sweet potatoes

1 ½ cups firmly packed light brown sugar, divided

¾ cup (1 ½ sticks) salted butter, divided

1 ¼ tsp. ground cinnamon, divided

¾ tsp. grated nutmeg, divided

2 large eggs, beaten

½ cup half-and-half

2 Tbsp. bourbon

1 ½ cups crushed corn flakes

1 cup chopped pecans

1. Preheat the oven to 400°F. Grease a 9-by-13-inch baking dish and set aside. Prick the potatoes with a fork, and bake on a baking sheet for 1 hour, or until tender. Let stand until cool enough to handle and then peel. Reduce the oven temperature to 350°F.

2. Beat the warm sweet potatoes, ½ cup of the brown sugar, ½ cup of the butter, 1 teaspoon of the cinnamon, and ½ teaspoon of the nutmeg with an electric mixer. Beat in the eggs, half-and-half, and bourbon. Spoon the mixture into the prepared baking dish.

3. Combine the corn flakes, the pecans, the remaining 1 cup brown sugar, the remaining ¼ teaspoon cinnamon, and the remaining ¼ teaspoon nutmeg. Melt the remaining ¼ cup butter and stir into the mixture. Sprinkle over the sweet potato mixture and bake for 40 to 45 minutes, or until the topping is browned. Serve.

Edna's Green Beans

When I finally reached adulthood and left behind my irrational hatred of all beans and peas, I discovered how good really fresh green beans could be, especially as cooked by my grandmother Edna Mae. Her secret, and the secret of many Southern cooks, was creating a gorgeous bronze pot liquor made from onions slow-braised in bacon drippings. If I'm really busy, I'll buy the bags of trimmed green beans and dump them straight into the pot liquor. I feel sure my Gram would understand.

6 slices bacon, coarsely chopped

2 small onions, chopped

2 lb. green beans, trimmed

1 ¾ cups low-sodium chicken broth

1 tsp. dried dill

Salt and freshly ground pepper

1. Cook the bacon in a large, deep skillet over medium-high heat for 6 to 8 minutes, or until crisp. Using a slotted spoon, transfer the bacon to paper towels to drain, reserving the drippings in the skillet.

2. Sauté the onions in the bacon drippings for 8 minutes, or until tender and beginning to caramelize. Stir in the green beans, broth, and dill.

3. Cover, reduce the heat, and simmer for 20 minutes, or until the green beans are tender. Sprinkle with the bacon, season with the salt and pepper to taste, and serve.

Cranberry-Orange Chutney

Is it a chutney? A relish? A sauce? I leave that up to others to decide. I love this make-ahead dish so much that I usually double the recipe so I have plenty to slather on my turkey leftovers. And speaking of leftovers, I also love to heat this up the next day, stir in some chopped fresh rosemary, a smidgen of finely diced jalapeño, and freshly ground black pepper, and after it cools, turn it into a savory topper for crackers smeared with a bit of goat cheese.

1 navel orange

1 (12-oz.) bag fresh cranberries

½ cup pomegranate seeds

½ cup firmly packed light brown sugar

1 tsp. grated fresh ginger

1. Grate the zest from the orange and place in a saucepan. Using a sharp knife, remove the rind, including the bitter white pith, and section the orange. Coarsely chop the segments and add to the orange zest.

2. Stir in the cranberries, pomegranate seeds, brown sugar, ginger, and ½ cup water. Bring to a boil, then reduce the heat and simmer, uncovered, for 10 to 15 minutes, or until the cranberries pop and the sauce thickens. Let cool and then transfer to a bowl, cover, and refrigerate until ready to serve.

Mashed Potatoes and Great Gravy

Even though she once ran a family-style restaurant, Sue Hogan didn't cook fancy. My mother would have laughed and flicked cigarette ashes in your hair if you'd suggested she add something like an herb garnish or an appetizer to her repertoire. But she lived and cooked large—and delicious. I learned to make these two dishes from the gravy-and-mashed-potatoes ninja master. And over the years, when she wasn't looking, I added some twists of my own, which I'm sure, if she were still living, would earn me a pop upside the head with a wooden spoon. At the very least.

5 lb. Yukon Gold potatoes, peeled and cut into chunks

2 cloves garlic, peeled

½ cup (1 stick) salted butter

4 oz. cream cheese, softened

¼ cup milk, plus extra as needed

1 Tbsp. kosher salt

Freshly ground pepper

1 recipe Great Gravy (recipe below)

1. Bring the potatoes in salted water to cover to a boil in a large stockpot. Add the garlic, and simmer for about 20 minutes, or until the potatoes are tender.

2. Drain the potatoes and return to the pot. Add the butter, cream cheese, milk, salt, and pepper to taste and mash until combined and the butter is melted. Stir in additional milk if needed to loosen to the desired consistency. Serve with the gravy.

GREAT GRAVY

Tom Turkey pan drippings, (page 158) plus giblets and neck (optional)

6 Tbsp. instant flour (we tested with Wondra)

2 cups low-sodium chicken broth

¾ cup dry sherry or white wine

1 tsp. poultry seasoning

Kosher salt and freshly ground pepper

1. Place the roasting pan with the pan drippings over medium-high heat. Remove and chop the giblets and neck, if desired. Whisk in the flour, 1 tablespoon at a time, until the

roux becomes a thick paste. Gradually add the chicken broth, 1 cup at a time, and sherry, whisking until combined.

2. Bring to a boil and whisk constantly until the gravy is thickened, adding additional water or broth if the mixture is too thick.

3. Stir in the poultry seasoning, chopped giblets and neck, if using, and season with the salt and pepper to taste.

Pecan Pie

After visiting the famous Mrs. Wilkes' Dining Room in Savannah, my mother decided to borrow the concept for her own restaurant, which she called Mrs. Hogan's Dining Room. Eventually both my brothers, Johnny and Tim, joined her in the business. The restaurant was located in an old-time retirement hotel in downtown St. Petersburg and featured family-style dining. Mom's guests loved her desserts, especially her pies, and she could turn out flaky home-made crusts by the dozen—with supernatural ease—a skill which I, sadly, did not inherit. At Thanksgiving, everybody sitting around her table got their own favorite dessert. She always made a mince pie for family friend Dave Tighe. And I always got pecan, which I still love. Today, I buy frozen pie crusts and nobody knows the difference, especially since the pecans come from my college roomie Pam Deal Harrell's own trees.

1 refrigerated pie crust (or frozen deep-dish pie crust, thawed)

1 cup dark corn syrup

⅔ cup sugar

3 large eggs, beaten

⅓ cup (about ⅔ stick) salted butter, melted

1 tsp. vanilla extract

1 cup pecans

1. Preheat the oven to 350°F. Unroll the pie crust and fit it into a 9-inch deep-dish pie plate. Fold and crimp the edges. (Skip this step if using a frozen crust.)

2. Whisk the corn syrup, sugar, eggs, melted butter, and vanilla together in a medium bowl. Stir in the pecans.

3. Pour the mixture into the prepared crust and bake for 45 minutes, or until the filling is set. Let cool on a wire rack for about 1 hour. Serve.

Andy's Personal Pumpkin Pie

Our son, Andy, adores anything pumpkin, especially pie. Every fall when he was young, I would buy a small pie pumpkin, and together we would cut up the pumpkin, scoop out the seeds, and salt and roast them, and then roast the pumpkin flesh for pie. It was good, messy fun. Since he'd helped make the pie, he thought it only fair that it should be his own personal pie, which he always devoured, solo, over the course of the Thanksgiving weekend. Although I no longer take the trouble to make my own pumpkin filling from scratch, the personal pie tradition still holds, so it's a good thing that this pumpkin pie recipe produces enough filling for an adult Andy-sized pie, plus three mini pies that Molly and Griffin love to help make—and eat. If you buy refrigerated pie crusts, as I do, just roll out the dough on a well-floured surface, place the miniature 6-inch pie pans on the dough, and cut around them with a sharp knife, making sure to leave a ½-inch border.

For the pie:

2 refrigerated pie crusts

1 (15-oz.) can pumpkin puree

1 (12-oz.) can evaporated milk

1 ¼ cups firmly packed dark brown sugar

3 large eggs

1 ½ tsp. ground cinnamon

½ tsp. salt

½ tsp. ground ginger

¼ tsp. grated nutmeg

⅛ tsp. ground cloves

⅛ tsp. freshly ground pepper

Sweetened whipped cream for serving (optional)

For the gingersnap streusel:

16 gingersnap cookies, crushed

1 cup all-purpose flour

½ cup (1 stick) salted butter, melted

⅓ cup granulated sugar

⅓ cup firmly packed dark brown sugar

⅛ tsp. ground ginger

1. Preheat the oven to 425°F. Unroll the pie crusts and fit into two 9-inch pie plates or one 9-inch pie plate and three 6-inch miniature pie tins. Fold and crimp the edges. Place on a rimmed baking sheet.

2. Whisk the pumpkin puree, evaporated milk, brown sugar, eggs, cinnamon, salt, ginger, nutmeg, cloves, and pepper together in a medium bowl. Pour the filling into the pie crusts, filling each three-quarters full.

3. Bake for 25 minutes, or until the filling is set.

4. To make the streusel, stir all the ingredients together in a medium bowl.

5. Reduce the oven temperature to 350°F. Remove the pies from the oven and sprinkle with the streusel. Return to the oven and continue baking until the topping is browned and the pies are done, 10 minutes for small pies or 20 to 25 minutes for large pies, shielding the edges with aluminum foil if necessary to prevent overbrowning.

6. Let the pies cool on wire racks for 3 hours. Serve with whipped cream, if desired.

Christmas Brunch

At Molly and Griffin's insistence, Christmas morning (heck, every morning) starts early—especially at Ebbtide, because they are always anxious to hit the beach. Last year, we had such a mild winter on Tybee, the children went swimming the day after Christmas! We serve this menu whenever we have a crowd gathered in the morning, which is fairly often. Make the casserole the night before and take it out of the fridge at least one hour before baking. Or, if you'd rather, make the Shrimp and Grits instead. The fruit salad can be made the night before, too. Since we all have a sweet tooth, and Christmas calories don't count (right?), we serve a decadent Cinnamon Roll Bread Pudding, too. And because it's Christmas, and an old tradition, I have a batch of Red Rooster Cocktails, a fruity, vodka-kissed slushie cocktail, in the freezer, ready to be mixed with ginger ale. Needless to say, we have mandated mid-morning naps for EVERYBODY after all the gifts are opened.

SERVES 6 TO 8

menu

Beachy Bloody Marys

Shrimp and Grits

Coconut-Rum Fruit Salad

Cinnamon Roll Bread Pudding

Red Rooster Cocktails

Jeanne's Breakfast Casserole

Beachy Bloody Marys

It was my brilliant garden- and chemistry-minded friend Linda Christian who came up with this solution for a quick and tasty Bloody Mary. "Why not add some of that bottled cocktail sauce we use for shrimp boils to the tomato juice?" she asked. "It's got all the stuff we put into a Bloody Mary: horseradish, celery salt, cayenne, pepper, Worcestershire . . . " Gadzooks! She was right. We always seem to have an opened bottle of cocktail sauce hanging around in the fridge at the beach. To make the cocktails even more festive, we rub the rims of the glasses with a slice of lemon and dip them in Old Bay seasoning. Here's a recipe for a whole pitcher of zesty lip-smacking beachies.

4 cups tomato juice or vegetable juice cocktail

1 cup vodka, or as desired

½ cup cocktail sauce

Hot sauce

¼ cup Old Bay seasoning

1 Tbsp. grated lemon zest plus 1 slice lemon

Cocktail onions, pickled okra, cooked bacon slices, celery sticks, pimento-stuffed olives, lemon slices for garnish (optional)

1. Combine the tomato juice, the desired amount of vodka, the cocktail sauce, and the hot sauce to taste in a large pitcher.
2. Combine the Old Bay and lemon zest on a shallow plate. Rub eight glasses with a lemon slice and dip each glass in the Old Bay mixture.
3. Pour the Bloody Marys into ice-filled glasses, and garnish as desired. Serve.

Shrimp and Grits

The first time I ever encountered this dish was when Tom and I were newlyweds. We were staying with my friend Jacky and her husband, who happened to be Tom's boss. The tide and the moon were right, so the boss invited Tom to go out shrimping in the tidal creeks behind their house, which turned out to be an all-night outing. In the morning, Jacky and I joined the guys in heading a 52-quart cooler full of shrimp. As a special treat, the boss decided to make us a real Savannah breakfast. The cheese grits sounded delightful, and the skillet with chopped bacon was also promising. Then, to my complete and utter horror, he proceeded to add shrimp to the pan! Shrimp for breakfast seemed like an absolutely barbaric concept. It took me years to get over my aversion to this dish. But somehow, I did. I recently made this for Andy and five of his best fishing buddies for breakfast (after I made them peel and devein the shrimp)—to raves. My version makes a slightly soupy shrimp gravy to pour over the grits. If you like less sauce, just cut back on the amount of chicken broth. Use wild-caught shrimp if you can, and always, always, put your guests to work with the deveiner!

2 ½ to 3 ½ cups low-sodium chicken broth

2 cups half-and-half

1 cup stone-ground grits

2 cups freshly grated Parmesan cheese

¼ cup (½ stick) salted butter

Salt and freshly ground black pepper

6 slices bacon

1 cup finely chopped sweet onion

1 small red bell pepper, chopped

1 jalapeño chile, seeded and minced (optional)

1 clove garlic, minced

2 lb. large shrimp, peeled and deveined

Juice of 1 lemon

2 Tbsp. chopped fresh parsley for garnish

2 Tbsp. chopped chives for garnish

1. Bring 2 ½ cups of the broth and the half-and-half to a boil in a medium saucepan over medium-high heat. Stir in the grits. Reduce the heat to low and cook, covered, for 15 to 20 minutes, or until the grits are tender and thickened. Remove from the heat and stir in the cheese and butter. Season with salt and pepper to taste. Cover and keep warm.

2. Cook the bacon in a large skillet over medium-high heat for 6 to 8 minutes, or until crisp. Transfer the bacon to paper towels to drain, reserving the drippings in the skillet. Crumble the bacon.

3. Sauté the onion, bell pepper, and jalapeño chile, if using, in the bacon drippings over medium heat for 5 minutes, or until tender. Add the garlic and cook for 1 minute longer.

4. Increase the heat to medium-high. Add ¼ cup of the broth and stir with a wooden spoon to loosen any browned bits from the skillet, adding additional broth, if necessary. Add the shrimp and sauté for 3 to 4 minutes, or until the shrimp turn pink.

5. Remove the pan from heat and stir in the lemon juice, crumbled bacon, and salt and pepper to taste. Spoon the shrimp mixture over the grits, sprinkle with the parsley and chives, and serve.

Coconut-Rum Fruit Salad

Growing up in Florida, practically everybody I knew had at least one kind of citrus tree in their yards, and we kids were not above poaching the occasional orange from a neighbor's tree or pelting each other with calamondins. These days, I buy those jars of mixed citrus fruits with grapefruit and orange sections in the refrigerated section at my supermarket and save myself the trouble of sectioning the fruit. Thawed frozen berries are perfectly acceptable to use here if fresh ones are out of season, and of course, you can sub in any other fruit you like. Just make sure you have enough citrus juice to keep the bananas from turning brown.

1 (20-oz.) jar refrigerated citrus segments

1 pineapple, peeled, cored, and cut in chunks

1 qt. strawberries, hulled and cut in half

1 pt. blueberries

2 bananas, sliced

1 cup green grapes, halved

¼ cup dark rum

1 cup sweetened flaked coconut, toasted

1. Drain the citrus segments and place in a serving bowl, reserving ½ cup juice. Add the pineapple, strawberries, blueberries, bananas, and grapes, tossing well with the reserved citrus juice to coat.

2. Stir in the rum. Cover and refrigerate until ready to serve. Sprinkle with the toasted coconut just before serving.

Cinnamon Roll Bread Pudding

Two of Tom's favorite grocery-store breakfast treats are cinnamon rolls—those big, gooey ones you buy on a foil tray in the bakery department—and apple fritters. So this is what you would get if an apple fritter were to marry a stale cinnamon roll. Not that a cinnamon roll was ever allowed to go stale in our house. But if that were to happen, you would have a heavenly culinary marriage—not to mention a very grateful audience around the breakfast table.

For the pudding:

½ cup raisins

¼ cup rum or brandy

2 cups half-and-half

1 cup firmly packed light brown sugar

⅔ cup milk

5 large egg yolks

2 tsp. vanilla extract

1 tsp. ground cinnamon

1 tsp. grated nutmeg

Pinch of salt

8 large cinnamon rolls, left uncovered overnight

2 cups peeled, chopped tart apples (such as Honey Crisp, Pink Lady, or Granny Smith)

½ cup finely chopped pecans

2 Tbsp. (¼ stick) unsalted butter, cut into pieces

1 ½ Tbsp. cinnamon sugar

For the icing:

½ cup powdered sugar

4 tsp. milk

½ tsp. white rum

1. Preheat the oven to 350°F. Butter a 7-by-11-inch casserole dish. Combine the raisins and rum and let stand for 30 minutes. Drain, reserving 1 teaspoon of the rum.

2. Beat the half-and-half, brown sugar, milk, egg yolks, vanilla, cinnamon, nutmeg, and salt together in a large bowl until well combined.

3. Cut the cinnamon rolls into 1-inch chunks and add to the egg mixture, tossing well to coat. Stir in the apples, raisins, pecans, and reserved rum. Let stand for 30 minutes or until the bread has absorbed most of the liquid.

4. Spoon the mixture into the prepared baking dish, dot with the butter, and sprinkle with the cinnamon sugar. Place the baking dish in a roasting pan. Pour boiling water into the roasting pan to reach halfway up the sides of the dish. Bake for 50 to 55 minutes, or until the bread pudding is set and the top is browned. Carefully remove the bread pudding from the water bath.

5. To make the icing, whisk the powdered sugar, milk, and rum in a small bowl until smooth. Drizzle the pudding with the icing and serve warm.

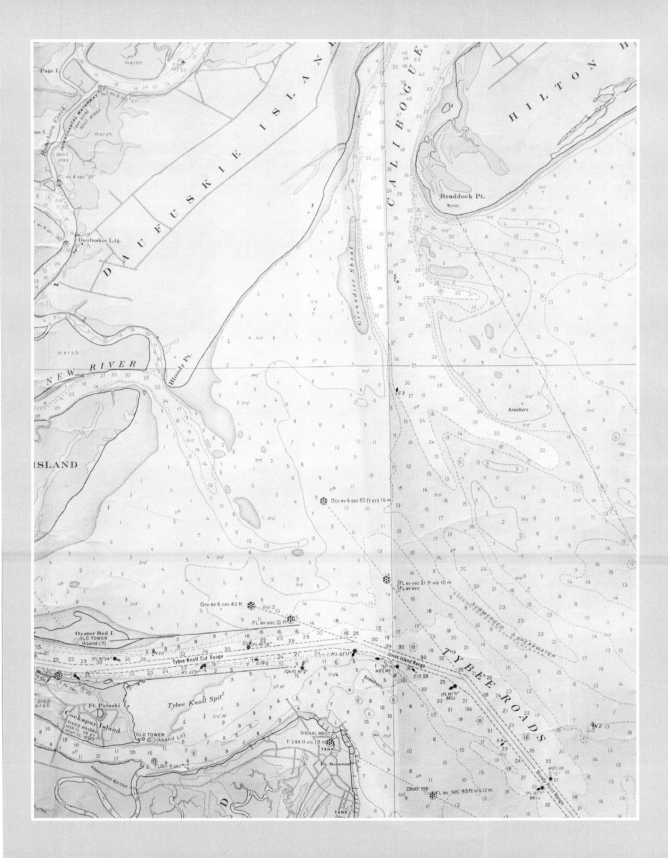

Jeanne's Breakfast Casserole

The hardest thing about this recipe is remembering to pick up frozen hash browns and green onions while I'm at the supermarket. Sliced deli ham really won't do for this recipe. You can buy packages of diced or cubed ham in the meat department, but if you have some leftover Easter or Christmas ham in the freezer, that elevates this dish to breakfast rock-star status. This is so easy, we frequently make it the night before, cover it with foil and refrigerate it, and then let it sit out on the counter to return to room temperature before baking. Do yourself a favor and beat the eggs in a large batter bowl with a spout, and then pour them into the baking dish when it's on the oven rack. I had to learn this lesson the hard way.

6 cups frozen hash brown potatoes

2 cups cubed ham

2 cups shredded pepper Jack cheese, divided

1 bunch green onions, chopped

1 (4-oz.) jar diced pimentos, drained

12 large eggs

1 (12-oz.) can evaporated milk

1 tsp. sea salt

½ tsp. freshly ground pepper

1. Preheat the oven to 350°F. Lightly grease a 9-by-13-inch baking dish. Spread the hash browns evenly in the baking dish, and then layer the ham, half of the cheese, the green onions, and the pimentos, in that order, on top of the hash browns.

2. Beat the eggs, evaporated milk, salt, and pepper together in a large batter bowl. Pour over the casserole and sprinkle with the remaining cheese.

3. Bake for 1 hour, or until the casserole is browned and the eggs are set. Cut into squares and serve hot or at room temperature.

New Year's Day Open House

We instituted our New Year's Day Open House more than twenty-five years ago, after I left my job as a newspaper reporter, as a good way to catch up with old friends and former colleagues we hadn't seen in a while. We decided to fashion the party after the oyster roasts we'd attended on Tybee, and augmented the menu with a huge baked ham that came to be affectionately known as "The Big-Ass Ham," and Tom's famous home-cured gravlax. In the South, good luck dishes like collard greens and black-eyed peas are a must-have on New Year's Day. My recipe for the grits and collard greens casserole was adapted to suit my lazy ways.
A newer version of the black-eyed peas is used in an easy-to-make Redneck Caviar. The open house became such a hit that the party grew by leaps and bounds, until one year we were astonished to realize the guest list had grown to nearly 300 names! When we eventually took a hiatus from the party, we actually had to send out "dis-invites" to warn people not to show up on New Year's Day. In recent years, we've reinstated the party at Ebbtide on a much smaller scale.

SERVES 10 TO 12

menu

Tom's Gravlax

Roast Oysters

Grits 'n' Greens Casserole

Redneck Caviar

Lemon–Cream Cheese Pound Cake

Tom's Gravlax

This herb-cured salmon always makes a command performance at our parties, especially around the holidays. We serve it very thinly sliced on dark pumpernickel bread, with traditional garnishes of red onion, capers, fresh dill, and a horseradish cream cheese or sour cream sauce. The prep itself is easy, but you'll need to give yourself at least a three-day head start to allow the salmon to cure.

½ cup coarse sea salt

½ cup coarsely ground pepper

⅓ cup sugar

1 (3-lb.) fillet wild-caught salmon (skin-on), cut in half crosswise

1 bunch fresh dill, plus dill sprigs for garnish

8 oz. cream cheese, softened

½ cup prepared horseradish

Salt and freshly ground pepper

1 (12-oz.) loaf party pumpernickel bread, toasted

Capers and sliced red onion for serving

1. Combine the salt, pepper, and sugar in a medium bowl. Sprinkle the flesh side of each piece of salmon with the salt mixture, covering the flesh entirely. Place the dill sprigs over the salt mixture and then press the salmon pieces together, flesh sides in.

2. Wrap the salmon tightly with plastic wrap. Place in a deep baking dish.

3. Place a cast-iron skillet or a pan lined with heavy cans on top of the salmon. Refrigerate for 3 days, turning the salmon every 12 hours. Discard any liquid at each turn.

4. Unwrap the salmon, remove the dill, and scrape off any remaining salt mixture. Thinly slice the salmon.

5. Beat the cream cheese and horseradish together until combined; season with salt and pepper to taste. Spread the cream cheese mixture on the toasted bread. Top with the sliced salmon, capers, onion, and remaining fresh dill sprigs and serve.

Roast Oysters

The first New Year's Day we owned Ebbtide, I decided to throw an oyster roast to show off our new beach house to friends and neighbors. Georgia coast, January, no problem getting oysters, right? Wrong. For two days, I called every seafood market, restaurant, and wholesaler all the way to Hilton Head Island, but everybody was sold out. In desperation, I put out a plea to my followers on Facebook, and sure enough, within thirty minutes, a sweet fan messaged me that her commercial oysterman husband's boat was tied up at the Lazaretto Creek dock ten minutes away, with plenty of just-caught oysters. Day. Saved. We prefer to grill over hardwood charcoal because it imparts a smoky flavor to the oysters, but plain charcoal or a gas grill will work.

4 to 6 dozen fresh oysters, scrubbed

Saltine crackers for serving

3 lemons, cut into wedges for serving

½ cup (1 stick) salted butter, melted

Hot sauce

Prepare a charcoal grill to high heat. After the coals are white, spread the oysters on the grill rack in a single layer. Cover with the grill lid and grill for 3 to 4 minutes, or until oysters have slightly popped open. Serve with the crackers, lemons, melted butter, and hot sauce.

Grits 'n' Greens Casserole

Even people who claim to dislike collard greens and/or grits are usually converted after one taste of this dish. I found the original recipe years ago in Southern Living *magazine and tweaked it over the years. I even included the recipe in the back of one of my most popular novels,* Hissy Fit, *which is appropriate, because friends now threaten to pitch a hissy if it doesn't show up on New Year's Day or as my contribution at a potluck.*

8 cups chicken broth, divided

2 cups half-and-half

2 cups stone-ground grits

2 ½ cups freshly grated Parmesan
   cheese, divided

1 cup (2 sticks) salted butter

½ tsp. freshly ground pepper

Salt

1 lb. collard greens, stemmed and
   chopped

8 slices bacon, cooked and crumbled

1. Preheat the oven to 350°F. Grease a 3-quart baking dish. Bring 6 cups of the chicken broth and the half-and-half to a boil in a large stockpot. Gradually stir in the grits. Return to a boil. Cover, reduce the heat, and simmer for 25 to 30 minutes, stirring frequently, until the grits are tender and the liquid is absorbed. Stir in 2 cups of the cheese, the butter, and the pepper. Season with salt to taste, and set aside.

2. Combine the remaining 2 cups broth and the collards in a Dutch oven. Bring to a boil. Reduce the heat and simmer for 10 minutes, or until the collards are tender. Drain well and press the collards with a paper towel to remove excess liquid.

3. Fold the cooked greens into the grits and spoon the mixture into the prepared baking dish. Sprinkle with the remaining cheese and the crumbled bacon.

4. Bake for 30 minutes, or until browned and bubbly. Serve.

Redneck Caviar

This dip is easy, healthy, and addictive. Serve it with corn chips or, healthier still, scoop it up with celery and yellow or red pepper triangles.

2 (15.5-oz.) cans black-eyed peas, drained and rinsed

1 (10-oz.) can diced tomatoes with green chiles, drained

1 small yellow bell pepper, diced

½ red onion, diced

½ cup sliced pickled okra

½ cup chopped fresh cilantro

½ cup olive oil

¼ cup apple cider vinegar

Corn chips for serving

1. Combine the black-eyed peas, tomatoes, bell pepper, onion, okra, and cilantro in a large bowl.

2. Whisk the oil and vinegar together in a separate bowl and stir into the black-eyed pea mixture. Serve with the corn chips.

Lemon–Cream Cheese Pound Cake

No Southern cook should be without a pound cake recipe in their repertoire. This recipe originated with my late sister Susie, who got it from her emergency room coworkers at Grady Memorial Hospital in Atlanta. Later, on the advice of famed food chemist Shirley Corriher, I upped the moistness ante with the addition of extra egg yolks, vegetable oil, and sugar. Bake it low and slow, and you'll have a triumph.

7 large eggs, divided

3 ¼ cups granulated sugar

1 ¼ cups (2 ½ sticks) salted butter, softened

8 oz. cream cheese, softened

¼ cup vegetable oil

1 tsp. lemon extract

1 tsp. vanilla extract

3 cups cake flour

¼ tsp. salt

Powdered sugar, sweetened whipped cream, and lemon zest curls for garnish (optional)

1. Preheat the oven to 325°F. Grease and flour a Bundt pan; set aside.

2. Separate the eggs, reserving 5 egg whites and 7 egg yolks in separate bowls. (Save the extra whites for another use.) Beat the egg whites at high speed with an electric mixer until stiff peaks form. Set aside.

3. Beat the sugar, butter, cream cheese, and oil with an electric mixer until fluffy. Add the egg yolks, one at a time, beating until the yellow disappears. Beat in the extracts.

4. Combine the flour and salt. Add the flour mixture to the butter mixture in three additions. Gently fold in the whipped egg whites.

5. Pour the batter into the prepared pan. Bake for 1 hour and 25 minutes, or until a wooden pick inserted in the center comes out clean. Let the cake cool in the pan for 5 minutes. Remove from the pan and transfer to a wire rack and let cool completely. Cut into slices, garnish with powdered sugar, whipped cream, and lemon zest, if desired, and serve.

Valentine's Day Sweetheart Dinner

The first year after we'd finished the renovation of the Breeze Inn, three of our favorite Atlanta couples came down over Valentine's Day weekend for a house party. Since the restaurant options back then were fairly limited, the husbands volunteered to cook an elegant dinner for the wives. Over the years, the guys have upped their epicurean game considerably, and the location varies from house to house—sometimes Atlanta, sometimes Tybee. Last year, at our friends the Tresslers', the printed menu, designed by our talented graphic artist friend Don Connelly, was so hysterical that we all had copies framed for posterity.

SERVES 6

menu

Sizzling Garlic Shrimp

Pork Medallions with Cherry-Balsamic
Pan Sauce

Scalloped Potatoes

Braised Brussels Sprouts

Chocolate Panna Cotta with
Strawberry Coulis

Sizzling Garlic Shrimp

We first tasted a Spanish-inspired dish called Gambas al Ajillo *at a restaurant in Raleigh, where it was served as an appetizer, and then again at a restaurant near our home in Atlanta, that serves it as an appetizer or an entrée. Tom set out to re-create it at home, and I think he succeeded. If you're planning this as a main dish, double the quantity and serve with rice or orzo. Either way, make sure you have plenty of crusty bread to sop up the garlicky juices.*

½ cup olive oil

10 cloves garlic, very thinly sliced

Juice of 1 large lemon

2 Tbsp. dry white wine

2 tsp. paprika

½ to 1 tsp. crushed red pepper (more
   if you like it super-spicy)

½ tsp. kosher salt

½ tsp. freshly ground black pepper

2 lb. medium or large shrimp, peeled
   and deveined

2 Tbsp. chopped fresh parsley

1 loaf crusty French bread for serving

1. Heat the oil in a large cast-iron skillet over medium heat. Add the garlic and sauté for 30 seconds, or until tender. Add the lemon juice, wine, paprika, crushed red pepper, salt, and black pepper.

2. Stir in the shrimp and cook for 2 to 3 minutes, or until the shrimp turn pink. Stir in the parsley, and serve hot with the French bread.

Pork Medallions with Cherry-Balsamic Pan Sauce

Pork tenderloins lend themselves to so many tasty, fast recipes, it's hard to pick just one favorite. But this one, with the pork sliced into medallions and then drizzled with a beautiful and savory cherry-balsamic sauce, always impresses. We also love this sauce on tiny baby lamb chops cooked with the same method.

3 (1-lb.) pork tenderloins

Kosher salt and freshly ground
    pepper

2 Tbsp. (¼ stick) unsalted butter

2 Tbsp. olive oil

1 small shallot, minced

4 cloves garlic, minced

½ cup balsamic vinegar

1 (13-oz.) jar cherry preserves

1 Tbsp. chopped fresh rosemary

1 Tbsp. grainy brown mustard

1. Preheat the oven to 400°F. Rub the pork with a generous sprinkling of salt and pepper.

2. Heat the butter and oil in a large, deep skillet over medium-high heat until hot. Working in batches if necessary, brown the pork tenderloins on all sides, 6 to 7 minutes. Transfer the tenderloins to a roasting pan, and bake for 10 to 15 minutes or to the desired doneness (about 135°F to 140°F for medium rare). Let rest for 10 minutes.

3. Meanwhile, add the shallot to the drippings in the skillet, and cook over medium heat for 1 minute, or until tender. Add the garlic and cook for 1 minute longer. Add the vinegar and stir with a wooden spoon, scraping the bottom of the skillet to loosen the pan drippings. Reduce the heat to low, and stir in the preserves, rosemary, and mustard. Cook, stirring occasionally, for 10 minutes, or until the sauce reduces and thickens. Season with salt and pepper to taste.

4. Slice the pork into ½-inch-thick slices and serve with the sauce.

Scalloped Potatoes

I can't think of a single potato recipe I don't love, but I really, really love scalloped potatoes. When I served this at a dinner party to celebrate the completion of our new kitchen in Atlanta, our guests were sneaking back into the kitchen for seconds and thirds. I'd say that's a success! The richness of this recipe calls for really good cheese—I like the nuttiness of Gruyère, plus the saltiness of freshly grated Parmesan. None of that pre-grated stuff from the green can, please!

4 lb. Yukon Gold potatoes, unpeeled and thinly sliced

¼ cup (½ stick) salted butter

3 cloves garlic, minced

¼ cup all-purpose flour

2 cups milk

1 cup chicken broth

2 cups shredded Gruyère cheese, divided

1 Tbsp. kosher salt

2 tsp. freshly ground pepper

1 onion, very thinly sliced

1 cup freshly grated Parmesan cheese

2 Tbsp. fresh thyme leaves

1. Preheat the oven to 375°F. Grease a large oval baking dish. Place the sliced potatoes in a bowl of salted water.

2. Melt the butter in a saucepan over medium heat; add the garlic and cook for 1 minute. Whisk in the flour and cook for 2 minutes, or until foamy. Gradually stir in the milk and cook for 5 minutes, stirring constantly, until the mixture begins to thicken. Whisk in the chicken broth and continue cooking until thickened. Add 1 cup of the Gruyère and stir until melted. Stir in the salt and pepper.

3. Drain the potatoes and pat dry with paper towels. Layer half of the potatoes in the bottom of the prepared baking dish. Top with half of the onion and half of the cheese sauce. Sprinkle with ½ cup Gruyère, ½ cup Parmesan, and 1 tablespoon of the thyme. Repeat the layers once.

4. Bake for about 1 hour, or until the potatoes are tender when pierced with a knife, shielding with foil if necessary to prevent overbrowning. Serve.

Braised Brussels Sprouts

The people who perpetrated frozen Brussels sprouts on post-war America have a lot to answer for, as far as I'm concerned. Mushy, stinky, gray-green—they turned off my whole generation to what is actually a gorgeous, delicious green treat. Thanks to some revisionist chef who spread the gospel of lightly braised, glazed fresh Brussels sprouts, this is now one of my family's favorite dishes, especially in fall and winter when they are plentiful in markets. When I find bags of shredded sprouts, I love to cook them this way and add in a handful of dried cranberries or cherries. Whatever you do, cook the sprouts just until tender.

6 slices applewood smoked bacon	2 lb. Brussels sprouts, trimmed
2 Tbsp. olive oil (optional)	1 cup low-sodium beef broth
½ cup chopped red onion	¼ cup balsamic vinegar

1. Cook the bacon in a large skillet over medium-high heat for 6 to 8 minutes, or until crisp. Transfer the bacon to paper towels to drain, reserving the drippings in the skillet. Crumble the bacon and set aside.

2. Add the oil to the bacon drippings, if necessary, and sauté the onion for 5 minutes, or until tender. Add the Brussels sprouts to the pan and stir well to coat. Add the broth; cover and cook for 5 minutes. Uncover and braise for 3 to 5 minutes longer, or until the Brussels sprouts are just barely tender and almost all the liquid has evaporated.

3. Remove the Brussels sprouts from the pan, and keep warm. Add the vinegar to the skillet, and cook over medium heat for 5 minutes, or until syrupy. Remove the pan from the heat, return the Brussels sprouts to the pan, and toss to coat well. Sprinkle with the bacon and serve warm.

Chocolate Panna Cotta with Strawberry Coulis

This sounds like a very fancy-Nancy recipe, but it's really simple—sort of an Italian chocolate pudding made without egg yolks, topped with a fast and delicious fresh strawberry sauce. Feel free to use any other berry that floats your gondola, though. I find those cute little glass custard cups at nearly every estate sale I go to, so I make my panna cotta in those, but it would also be pretty served in wineglasses or champagne coupes. Okay, let's be honest, it would taste just as good if you just left it in the bowl you prepared it in and passed around long-handled spoons. But that doesn't sound very romantic, now, does it?

For the panna cotta:

1 cup milk

1 (¼-oz.) envelope unflavored gelatin

2 cups whipping cream

½ cup sugar

5 oz. dark chocolate, chopped

1 tsp. espresso powder

½ tsp. vanilla extract

Sweetened whipped cream, chocolate shavings, strawberry halves for serving (optional)

For the strawberry coulis:

1 qt. strawberries, hulled and sliced

½ cup sugar

1 Tbsp. fresh lemon juice

1. Coat six 6-ounce glass custard cups with cooking spray, and dab away the excess with a paper towel. Pour the milk into a medium bowl and sprinkle with the gelatin. Let stand for 5 minutes, or until the gelatin softens.

2. Combine the cream and sugar in a heavy medium saucepan over medium-high heat and cook until the sugar dissolves. Bring to a boil, then remove from the heat. Add the chocolate and whisk until melted. Whisk the warm chocolate mixture into the gelatin mixture. Whisk in the espresso powder and vanilla.

3. Divide the mixture evenly between the custard cups. Cover and refrigerate for at least 6 hours.

4. To make the coulis, combine the strawberries, sugar, and lemon juice in a small sauce-pan, and mash the berries with a wooden spoon to release the juice. Cook over medium heat for 5 minutes, or until the sauce begins to bubble. Let cool.

5. Puree the sauce slightly, if desired. Refrigerate until ready to serve.

6. To serve, unmold each panna cotta onto a dessert plate. Top with the whipped cream, chocolate shavings, and strawberry halves, if desired, and serve with the coulis.

Easter Lunch

Easter was the first family holiday we celebrated with the family at the Breeze Inn, and we've been gathering the family together at Tybee on Easter ever since. Our church, St. Michael's, is only a stroll from both houses and was originally built by church members who were boat-builders. After Mass, we come home and hunt Easter eggs while Tom fires up the grill for his famous garlic-marinated leg of lamb. The menu varies according to my mood—and what friends arrive with covered dishes—but the lamb and the delicious medley of spring green vegetables, rice pilaf, and my mother's beloved carrot cake with maple–cream cheese frosting never vary.

SERVES 6

menu

Grilled Leg of Lamb

Ginger Spring Vegetables

Green Rice Pilaf

Mrs. Hogan's Carrot Cake

Grilled Leg of Lamb

I'd never eaten lamb until marrying into my husband's family, whose roots are in Eastern Europe. Together, over the decades, Tom and I have found and enjoyed half a dozen delicious preparations for lamb, in the process converting many friends who'd also never enjoyed lamb.

1 (5- to 6-lb.) bone-in leg of lamb

1 (24-oz.) container plain Greek yogurt

1 cup olive oil

Juice of 2 lemons

10 cloves garlic, smashed

3 Tbsp. chopped fresh rosemary

Freshly ground pepper and sea salt

1 Tbsp. instant flour (we tested with Wondra)

2 cups beef broth

1. Pat the lamb dry with paper towels. Place the lamb in an extra-large zip-top plastic bag.

2. Combine the yogurt, oil, lemon juice, garlic, rosemary, 2 tablespoons pepper, and 1 tablespoon salt in a medium bowl. Pour the mixture over the lamb, turning to coat, and marinate in the refrigerator at least 6 hours or overnight.

3. Remove the lamb from the marinade and wipe off the excess.

4. Prepare a charcoal or gas grill using the indirect heat method: Either rake the hot coals to one side of a charcoal grill or heat only one side of a gas grill to medium-hot.

5. Place the lamb on the grill grate over the hot side of the grill and sear on all sides until browned. Place the lamb in a metal baking pan and place over indirect heat. Cover with the grill lid and grill, turning the meat every 15 minutes, for 1 hour to 1 hour and 30 minutes, until a meat thermometer inserted in the thickest portion registers 140°F for medium-rare. Remove the lamb from the grill, tent with foil, and let rest for 30 minutes. Place the lamb on a rimmed cutting board to allow the juices to drain.

6. While the lamb rests, place the pan with the drippings over medium heat. Whisk in the flour, and cook for 2 minutes, or until foamy. Gradually add the broth and whisk until combined. Bring to a boil and cook for 5 minutes, or until thickened. Season with salt and pepper to taste.

7. Carve the lamb, and serve with the gravy.

Ginger Spring Vegetables

My college roommate didn't know how to cook when we moved into our first apartment together back in Athens, Georgia. Come to think of it, I didn't know much either, but I did know how to boil water, and she didn't. Nancy Kwan Hom, who is Chinese, eventually learned how to make her mother's stir-fried broccoli, which she shared with me. It was the inspiration for this lovely spring green medley.

8 oz. Broccolini, trimmed

8 oz. sugar snap or snow peas, trimmed

8 oz. asparagus, trimmed

1 red bell pepper, thinly sliced

2 Tbsp. cornstarch

2 Tbsp. low-sodium soy sauce

3 Tbsp. peanut oil

2 shallots, thinly sliced

1 tsp. grated fresh ginger

½ tsp. kosher salt

1. Bring a large pot of water to a boil. Add the Broccolini and cook for 2 to 3 minutes, or until crisp-tender. Remove from the water and plunge into an ice water bath.

2. Return the water to a boil. Add the sugar snap peas and cook for 1 to 2 minutes, or until crisp-tender. Remove from the water and add to the ice water bath.

3. Return the water to a boil. Add the asparagus and red bell pepper strips and cook for 2 to 3 minutes or until crisp-tender. Remove from the water and add to the ice water bath. Drain all the vegetables well.

4. Whisk the cornstarch with ¼ cup water and the soy sauce and set aside.

5. Heat the oil in a large skillet over medium heat. Add the shallots and sauté for 3 minutes. Add the ginger and sauté for 1 minute longer. Add the vegetables and salt, stirring well to coat. Add the cornstarch mixture and cook for 3 minutes, or until the sauce thickens. (Stir in additional water, if necessary, if the sauce becomes too thick.) Serve.

Green Rice Pilaf

This rice pilaf lightens up a fairly rich menu, and it's easy to make ahead and either keep warm or serve at room temperature. Save some time and buy a bag of matchstick carrots.

2 cups low-sodium chicken broth

1 cup jasmine rice

½ cup matchstick carrots

1 cup frozen peas

4 green onions, sliced

¼ cup chopped fresh parsley

2 Tbsp. (¼ stick) salted butter

½ tsp. salt

Freshly ground pepper

1. Bring the broth to a boil in a saucepan with a tight-fitting lid. Stir in the rice. Cover, reduce the heat, and simmer for 15 minutes, or until the liquid is absorbed and the rice is tender.

2. Meanwhile, place the carrots and 2 tablespoons water in a small microwave-safe bowl. Microwave on high power for 3 to 4 minutes, or until tender, and then drain.

3. Fluff the rice with a fork. Stir in the carrots, peas, green onions, parsley, butter, and salt, and season with the pepper to taste. Serve.

Mrs. Hogan's Carrot Cake

My mother must have baked hundreds of these super-moist three-layer cakes with maple–cream cheese frosting in her lifetime. It was a family favorite as well as the star of the dessert rotation at the restaurant she ran in downtown St. Petersburg. She probably burned through half a dozen food processors grating all those carrots. After Mom passed away, my sister Susie inherited the carrot cake tradition. One Christmas, Susie and I baked the cake layers and left them cooling on her kitchen counter. When we turned around, we discovered that Wyatt, our English setter, had devoured most of one of the layers. We mixed up another batch of batter, put it in the oven, and then realized we'd used up all the eggs we needed for another recipe. We set the timer and put my dad and Tom, who were watching football, in charge of removing the cakes. When we returned from the store, we were greeted with the distinctive aroma of burnt cake. Sure enough, their team had scored a couple of touchdowns—but our cakes were ruined. Again. That was the year we discovered that a two-layer carrot cake was better than none.

For the cake:

4 large eggs

1 cup vegetable oil

2 cups all-purpose flour

2 cups granulated sugar

2 tsp. baking soda

2 tsp. ground cinnamon

1 tsp. salt

4 cups grated carrots

½ cup finely chopped pecans

Carrots with tops, coarsely chopped
   pecans for garnish (optional)

For the frosting:

1 lb. cream cheese, softened

1 cup (2 sticks) unsalted butter,
   softened

2 tsp. vanilla extract

2 tsp. maple flavoring

2 lb. powdered sugar

1 to 2 Tbsp. milk (optional)

1. Preheat the oven to 350°F. Grease three 8-inch cake pans, and line the bottoms with parchment paper.

2. Beat the eggs and oil in a large bowl together with an electric mixer until frothy. Combine the flour, sugar, baking soda, cinnamon, and salt in a separate bowl. Gradually add the flour mixture to the egg mixture, beating until well combined. Stir in the grated carrots and chopped pecans.

3. Pour the batter into the prepared cake pans, and bake for 25 to 30 minutes, or until a wooden pick inserted in the center of a cake comes out clean. Remove the cakes from the pans, and let cool completely on wire racks.

4. To make the frosting, beat the cream cheese and butter with an electric mixer until creamy. Beat in the vanilla and maple flavoring.

5. Gradually add the powdered sugar, beating after each addition until combined. Beat in the milk, if necessary, to reach a spreadable consistency.

6. Spread the frosting between and on top of the cake layers. Garnish with carrots with tops and coarsely chopped pecans, if desired, and serve.

Epilogue

And Then There Were Biscuits

I thought I'd written everything I had to say about cooking at the beach. But then came a Sunday morning when my family was gathered around the table, laughing and joking and fighting over that last piece of bacon, and the realization came in a flash. Biscuits! You really can't have a Southern cookbook without including a great biscuit recipe.

Why? Because they are a little tricky to make. As a platform for bacon or a patty of sausage, as a late-afternoon snack with honey or jam, or at supper to sandwich a slab of fried chicken breast or to chase down and deliver the last bit of pot roast and gravy, biscuits are welcome on every occasion and at every table.

The trouble was, over the years, after some early failures at biscuit-making, I'd come to settle for OPB—other people's biscuits. First, I used Bisquick, then biscuits from a can, and more recently, frozen bagged biscuits, which I think come pretty close to greatness if you're pressed for time, or biscuit-impaired like me.

Finally, I was forced to confront my fear of biscuit-making. I tested half a dozen different recipes, consulted experts in the field (thanks, Facebook friends!), and worked on my technique. I went through a five-pound bag of self-rising flour and a quart of buttermilk in a single weekend—before Katie reminded me that we already had a superlative biscuit recipe given to us by someone whose memory we treasure.

Although most of the recipes in this cookbook emphasize easy, stress-free dishes, sometimes it really is worthwhile to do things the old-fashioned way. Sometimes it's okay to use the whole-fat buttermilk, to take the time to sift flour, and to dig out your grater to shred the frozen butter into just the right size. You discover that sprinkling flour on a countertop and gently shaping the dough to the right thickness before cutting out the biscuits and placing them lovingly into a greased pan can be a transformative experience. Suddenly, you're back at your mother's or grandmother's side, and their hands are guiding yours in a skill you didn't know you possessed.

And then the biscuits come out of the oven and you break one apart, still warm and steamy from the oven, and let a pat of golden butter dissolve on the surface. Maybe you add some preserves, or a piece of ham left over from last night's dinner. Or both.

Then the ultimate beauty of biscuits is revealed. Portability!

You take your biscuit, walk right down to the beach, and let your toes sink into the sand. Let the waves lap at your ankles and ponder how lucky you are to be at the beach and to taste the blessing of a humble biscuit, made with the simplest of ingredients: flour, buttermilk, butter, and your own two hands.

This, my friends, is beach house cooking.

Buttermilk Biscuits

When Katie and Mark got married a few years ago, I put together a cookbook of recipes and anecdotes from friends and family. One of the most anticipated contributions was from Elvita Hamm, my dear friend Susie's octogenarian mother, called Muvv, by all who loved her. Muvv's biscuit recipe called for buttermilk and White Lily flour, which is a soft wheat flour prized by generations of Southern cooks like Muvv, who said, "Katie, if you can't get self-rising White Lily at your store, it means you've moved too far from the South and you need to come home." Two keys to making a tender, flaky biscuit are using really cold, full-fat buttermilk and butter and handling the dough as little as possible. Muvv worked the fat into the flour using her hands, but since I don't have her deft touch, I use a pastry cutter. Muvv's final words on baking biscuits were these: "Place those biscuits around the inside of that greased pan and reserve space in the middle for that center biscuit that belongs solely to you." (Sorry about that, Mark.) This recipe makes about 7 biscuits.

2 cups self-rising soft wheat flour

½ cup (1 stick) unsalted butter, frozen and grated, plus melted butter for brushing

¾ cup buttermilk, very cold

All-purpose flour for dusting

1. Preheat the oven to 450°F. Grease a 9-inch cast-iron skillet.
2. Sift the self-rising flour into a large bowl and add the grated butter. Working quickly, cut the butter into the flour with two forks or a pastry blender until it's the size of peas. Drizzle the buttermilk over the flour mixture, and stir with a spatula just until the ingredients are moistened and form a ball.
3. Dust the counter with all-purpose flour, turn the dough out onto the counter, and dust the top with additional flour. Pat the dough into a rectangle about 1-inch thick. Cut into biscuits using a 2 ½- to 3-inch biscuit cutter, rerolling as needed to make seven biscuits. Place the biscuits in the prepared skillet, and brush the tops with melted butter.
4. Bake for 18 to 22 minutes, or until browned. Serve.

Acknowledgments

MARY KAY ANDREWS: This book is dedicated to Tom Trocheck, my starter husband of forty years, who catches, cleans, and cooks the seafood; grills the lamb; and chops the onions, and who is forever bickering, bossing, and contradicting me in the kitchen, but who always, no matter what, lights my fire both in and out of the kitchen.

In truth, the idea for a cookbook had been simmering for years on the back burners of my imagination. But it took the nagging of my old friend and creative genius Elizabeth Demos to bring the idea to fruition, especially since she'd already assembled the dream team of recipe writer and food stylist extraordinaire Ashley Strickland Freeman and virtuoso food photographer Mary Britton Senseney. The "girls" made this project more enjoyable and educational than I would have dared to hope, and my recipes have never looked more beautiful. My family—the one I was born into, the one I married into, and the one Tom and I have created together—Katie and Mark, Andy, and our adored grandchildren, Molly and Griffin, are always the inspiration for every dish I create. And the cherished friends with whom we've shared vacations, dinners, drinks, recipes, and laughs over the years—you all know who you are—add invaluable spice to our lives. To my publishing team—literary agent Stuart Krichevsky of SKLA; marketing guru and dear pal Meghan Walker of Tandem Literary; and the rock stars at St. Martin's Press: head cheerleader/publisher Sally Richardson, editor extraordinaire

Jennifer Enderlin, Jessica Lawrence, Tracey Guest, Erica Martirano, Brant Janeway, and especially art director Michael Storrings, who once again gave me a gorgeous cover—I send huge thanks and love.

ASHLEY STRICKLAND FREEMAN: I dedicate my work on this book to my husband, Chris—whose support and encouragement has allowed me to be "Mom" to our one-year-old son, Anderson, and to pursue my career at the same time. I owe a huge thanks to my fabulous coworkers and friends, Elizabeth Demos and Mary Britton Senseney, without whom this project would never have been possible, as well as to Bert John, our amazing production assistant who helped with everything from food prep and schlepping to comic relief and creative advice. And to my family—Anderson's Gigi, Pop, and Gramma—thank you for entertaining our little guy while I spent long days on set and for your continued support over the years. Finally, to Mary Kay Andrews: Thank you for the opportunity to work on this project, and for trusting me with your family recipes.

ELIZABETH DEMOS: I dedicate my work on this book to my husband, Paul, and son, William. I'd also like to recognize my treasure-hunting companions, Bert John and Mitchell Hall. They helped me scour antique shops, thrift stores, and estate sales in pursuit of the perfect props for this cookbook. I'd like to thank Bert for his tireless work as the production assistant for our team. Special thanks to Mitchell Hall, Genevieve Routon, and Meta Adler for their careful attention and talent on our cover shoot with MKA. Last, I'd like to thank Mary Kay Andrews, for believing in the project and my cookbook teammates, photographer Mary Britton Senseney and food stylist Ashley Strickland Freeman.

MARY BRITTON SENSENEY: I dedicate my work on this book to my mother, Sherrill Senseney, who taught me that anyone can become family around the dinner table. Thank you to Mary Kay Andrews, for trusting me with the photography for this project. Many thanks to our creative team, Elizabeth Demos, Ashley Strickland Freeman, and Bert John, for making work not feel like work. And to my husband, Chase: Thank you for keeping the home fires burning for our family. My work on this project wouldn't have been possible without you.

Index

About the Author

Mary Kay Andrews is the *New York Times* bestselling author of twenty-four novels, including *The Weekenders*, *Beach Town*, *Ladies' Night*, *Hissy Fit*, and *Savannah Breeze*. A former features writer for *The Atlanta Journal-Constitution*, she finds an outlet for her passion for cooking, entertaining, and decorating with vintage finds at the homes she shares in Atlanta and Tybee Island, Georgia, with her husband, Tom, and their two grown children, Katie and Andy, as well as grandchildren Molly and Griffin. This is her first cookbook